ABOUT THE BOOK

Attaining a valued leadership role requires more than technical skills. Interacting appropriately with everyone in the organization, while introducing or supporting tactical initiatives, is fundamental.

Concepts of Managing reveals essential lessons leaders must understand. Offering uniquely realistic portrayals of situations encountered in business, Ronald Harris' principles reveal beneficial concepts in action which empower workplace application. Utilizing this guidance—which is seasoned with candor and optimism—readers can anticipate scenarios and thoughtfully approach challenges. Armed with real-world wisdom, they will consequently experience fewer career detours and avoid the roughest waters. Furthermore, self-esteem and the respect of admirable peers will be cultured, increasing employment opportunities and heightening success.

This book speaks to supervisors and managers as well as aspiring workers, since everyone faces employment challenges. Harris' concepts are relevant to university students, employees in training programs, people in business, and those trying to succeed with limited access to mentoring resources.

CONCEPTS OF MANAGING

A ROAD MAP FOR AVOIDING CAREER HAZARDS

RONALD HARRIS

WITH:
JACQUELINE H. HARRIS, PhD
CASEY B. HARRIS, JD, MBA

authorHOUSE

AuthorHouse™
1663 Liberty Drive
Bloomington, IN 47403
www.authorhouse.com
Phone: 833-262-8899

© 2023 Ronald Harris. All rights reserved.

No part of this book may be reproduced, stored in a retrieval system, or transmitted by any means without the written permission of the author.

Published by AuthorHouse 10/16/2023

ISBN: 979-8-8230-1519-6 (sc)
ISBN: 979-8-8230-1518-9 (hc)
ISBN: 979-8-8230-1517-2 (e)

Library of Congress Control Number: 2023918274

Print information available on the last page.

Any people depicted in stock imagery provided by Getty Images are models, and such images are being used for illustrative purposes only.
Certain stock imagery © Getty Images.

This book is printed on acid-free paper.

Because of the dynamic nature of the Internet, any web addresses or links contained in this book may have changed since publication and may no longer be valid. The views expressed in this work are solely those of the author and do not necessarily reflect the views of the publisher, and the publisher hereby disclaims any responsibility for them.

DEDICATION

There have been so many family members, friends, and work associates who deserve to be mentioned in this dedication. My hope is that they won't feel hurt or overlooked when I only mention two of them, because of their significant roles in bringing this work to realization.

I offer my deepest love and appreciation to my wife of over 48 years. She has stood at my side as a much more-than-equal partner through all of life's challenges. She is still—and will always be—the woman of my dreams. As the song "Heartbreaker" by Dionne Warwick offers, "This world may end, not you and I."[1]

I also want to express my heartfelt gratitude to Carl Daniels, my most influential mentor. He invested countless hours helping me understand how to conduct business in a thoughtful and effective manner. The wisdom he shared permeates this book. He remains a dear friend through thick and thin.

---

[1] Warwick, Dionne. "Heartbreaker." *AZ Lyrics*. 2008. lyrics.com/lyric/14638845/Dionne+Warwick/Heartbreaker. Accessed 11 April 2023.

FOREWORD

Leadership and management are essential skills for anyone looking to succeed in business or any other field. Whether you're a small business owner, a leader of a diverse team, or a manager at a large corporation, having the ability to lead and manage effectively is crucial to your success and the success of your team and organization.

Ron was my first exposure to what I later realized was executive coaching. He was the first leader in my career. I was introduced to him when I joined a clothing retail company in their distribution and logistics operations. I worked for that firm for ten years, and while Ron wasn't there the whole time, he continued to encourage and coach me. Years later, Ron recruited me to another firm, and I had three more wonderful years working closely with him and learning from him. I found him to be consistent as he strove to apply the principles in this book during his executive leadership in the company, although he would readily acknowledge any need for improvement. My leadership style is strongly influenced by his mentoring to this day.

In this book, Ron explores the key concepts of common sense in leadership and management, from establishing personal credibility, setting clear goals and expectations, to building strong teams, and fostering a positive culture. Ron delves into the different qualities of leadership and how to choose those that are right for you to work on, as well as the importance of effective communication and decision-making.

Throughout the book, Ron provides real-world examples and practical tips for applying these concepts in the workplace. Whether you're just starting out in your career or you're an experienced manager looking to sharpen your skills, this book is a valuable resource for anyone looking to improve their leadership and management abilities.

With its comprehensive coverage of key concepts, this book is a must-read for anyone looking to take their career to the next level. So why wait? Start learning and improving your leadership and management skills today!

Jeff Lamb
V.P. of Human Resources, SPHR

PREFACE

Managing: "[t]o handle or direct with a degree of skill: such as to exercise executive, administrative, and supervising direction."[2] Throughout my career, I have increasingly observed and analyzed the causes of positive and negative outcomes in the workplace. My intent is to make recommendations that when thoughtfully applied will provide the reader a roadmap to avoid career hazards and experience greater success instead. This includes sharing lessons I learned the hard way and reminding myself of the values I've labored to incorporate in my approach to life and business. My hope is that while reading this book you will conclude that I'm not trying to put myself on a pedestal, since I would fall off anyway. The associates I've worked with over the years could relate times when I haven't lived up to the principles that are shared in the pages that follow. Rather, try to learn from my mistakes—and occasional successes—so you don't have to experience any undesirable consequences yourself. Over the years, I've referred to myself on occasion as a "slow study": I eventually get it, but not quickly.

I recall sitting with coworkers on several occasions and saying we ought to write a book someday. This almost always followed an episode that was handled poorly or went wrong because someone else in the organization didn't perform up to our expectations (of course, those we were critiquing might have had frustrations with how we handled our own duties).

Around 1995, I was teaching a course on supervision as an adjunct

---

[2] "Managing." *Merriam-Webster*, 2023, merriam-webster.com/dictionary/managing. Accessed 27 February 2023.

professor for Penn State at the Berks County Campus. As we neared the end of the course, I felt like the textbook in use hadn't addressed many topics that should have been included between the covers. So, for our last session together, I developed a list of those overlooked issues. That document was the focus of our final class discussion and became the genesis for this book. Over the next twenty-five plus years, that list was enhanced and amplifications were added as ideas came to my mind while training staff or teaching. You might say I finally got around to putting it down on paper.

You've heard it said that there's nothing as uncommon as common sense. It's increased by experience and deductive reasoning. We not only learn from our own mistakes and successes, but also from observing people whose paths we cross: it's far less painful and much more efficient. Most of the insights contained within this book were neither initially nor exclusively mine, but I acquired them and can now attest to their value, having proved them for myself. Think of this book as lending the reader advice given to me by successful managers and authors who were willing to invest the time and effort to coach me along the way. Undoubtedly, you may have heard some of these principles before, perhaps in slightly different terms and from more accomplished individuals. Hopefully, you've already applied many of these precepts and have come to personally believe in their worth. Maybe hearing them again with a new slant will help you adopt more of these as your own. This might be the first time you've been exposed to many of them.

These principles have universal application. Please don't discount them because of the situation-specific examples offered. Forgive me for sharing the expanse of my employment to help confirm that assertion. I didn't build a billion-dollar empire from scratch. However, to the best of my knowledge, I've worked in management for at least seven firms with sales ranging from $90 million to $3 billion and with four others having assets or holdings equaling or exceeding those figures. This experience spans numerous industries including agriculture, banking, commercial real estate, construction, consulting, direct sales/multi-level marketing, higher education, and retail. During that time, I've administered a wide variety of disciplines such as buying/purchasing, collections, facilities, inventory control, manufacturing, operations (including in-house medical and food services), order fulfillment, project management, quality assurance/control, receiving, R&D, shipping, store management, transportation, and warehousing.

Even though you may never work in a retail store or warehouse, someday you may find that understanding one of the different disciplines or operations discussed in these pages is very valuable. You may even find yourself responsible for that area. Case in point: an executive with a strong financial background once asked me who in the distribution division was responsible for the undesirable mushrooming inventory levels in the company. It became necessary to explain that the warehouse staff only received, stored, and shipped what was sent to them by the purchasing department. If the executives wanted to start thoughtfully lowering the inventory, it would depend upon the merchandise analysts who provided the purchasing agents with their open-to-buy financial targets. It was this group that tracked sales in relation to on-hand inventory in order to determine what dollar level of raw materials and finished goods would result in the desired annual inventory turns. Shouldn't that leader have understood these concepts in their influential role?

Keeping in mind that my perception of what happened is often different from that of others involved, I've spent a great deal of time concerned with using examples involving coworkers in this book. Regarding any stories or illustrations that might shed a negative light on someone else, some facts have been fictionalized (including gender, title, or setting) to avoid offending or disparaging them. My sincere hope is that in the spirit of letting others learn from our missteps, the anonymity of the stories will prevent anybody from becoming angry or embarrassed. These experiences are neither to be taken as an indictment against someone, nor to discredit a successful career. You are, however, welcome to critique my personal mistakes, since as this stage of my life I no longer have any delusions of grandeur.

While working back east, I remember discussing with my boss how both of our fathers made their living and how that may have put us at a disadvantage trying to be successful in management professions. That's not to suggest that we didn't have the necessities of life plus a good home environment and occasional indulgences that were frosting on the cake. As I recall, my boss' dad was an electrician. My dad did many different things: when he was a young man, he was a heavy equipment operator (bulldozers, graders, etc.) and then became a construction supervisor and then foreman. He later owned a gasoline service station, tried his hand as a real estate agent, supervised a maintenance shop for heavy equipment, and was a property appraiser for the state. Both of our fathers' backgrounds were primarily blue-collar. My boss speculated that since we didn't sit around the dinner table listening to our parents discuss how to navigate the boardroom and corporate corridors, we lacked a leg up in our careers which others might have been given. In fact, my dad once joked to me, "Son, do you want to make a million dollars? Okay, then work a million hours." If you also consider that I was raised in a time when children were to be seen and not heard, maybe you can understand my timidity to assert myself, especially with people who were supervisors or my elders. Einstein once wrote, "Blind obedience to authority is the greatest enemy of truth."[3] Even today, I find myself occasionally intimidated by a powerful authority figure.

That said, from day one on the job I was aware of inconsistencies in how people managed others, and as a young idealist I wanted to improve the workplaces where I found myself. My college degrees were financed by working—holding three part-time jobs at one point—and by loans. There were a few semesters when I lived at home or in an extra bedroom

---

[3] In a letter to Jost Winteler dated July 8, 1901. Quoted in *The Ultimate Quotable Einstein*. Edited by Alice Calaprice, Princeton University Press, 2011. p. 161.

at the home of my brother and sister-in-law. For this free room and board, I remain very grateful. While going through my master's program, I was newly married and working full time, which wasn't a very wise decision (the working part). My determination to attend graduate school in organizational behavior was intended to prepare me to successfully function in several disciplines including human relations, management, and consulting. Since we were in the same graduate school as the MBAs and MPAs, sometimes we found ourselves taking the same courses. My wish was that there had been a few courses in college (both while attending and teaching) where the topics in this manuscript could have been discussed at length. Even though professors may not agree with many of my positions, perhaps this book might become a resource for use in some classes, if for nothing else than to stimulate discussion.

Over time, it became my inclination to shy away from the consultant option recognizing I hadn't yet "been there" nor "done that." Within my mind was a feeling I couldn't get past, believing years and years of personal experience were required before making recommendations on how others should manage. How could a consultant give sound advice when they hadn't been through the very challenge their clients were facing? Now, here I am with 50 years of relevant experience, finally feeling like there's wisdom to share but praying it will be welcomed. Of course, my hope is that the reader will be contemplative in applying any concepts to their personal situations.

Rereading the manuscript numerous times, I've wondered what my critics might say. Realizing the words written have a very common feel when viewed in their entirety, what tone do the contents of this book impart or convey? Is it idealistic, pessimistic, realistic, optimistic, or what? My desire is that this book comes across as realistic with a generous dose of optimism. I hope it's realistic in that it acknowledges the ups and downs encountered in my working years. It's not intended to paint the picture that if you use a few silver bullets everything will come up roses.

It's optimistic in the sense that if you approach each challenge with an arsenal of acquired learning and try to take the high road, things will work out much more often.

It became apparent during my revisions that many of the subjects discussed are interrelated. The analogy of how multiple interwoven threads create an attractive fabric also applies to how good judgment and skill helps produce the best managers. Please forgive the use of less politically-desirable terms such as coworker, employee, and subordinate as an effort to not overuse more appropriate terms such as staff member or team member to the point of distraction. For similar purposes titles like supervisor, manager, director, and boss are used interchangeably.

Take this book for what it's worth: one man's career-long reflections living in or near the trenches, intended to give a helping hand to those who want to break through into a managerial role and attempt to be successful in their assignments. May the contents of this book especially help young people as they try to make progress in their profession. If they've anticipated situations and have guidelines to fall back upon, they'll experience fewer detours along their charted course and can avoid the roughest waters. While it doesn't contain a formula for becoming wealthy, this book is intended to culture self-respect and the esteem of those peers you admire, which in turn should increase your employability and compensation while affording you some peace of mind.

After reading my offering, some critics might argue that many of the managerial concepts are signs of weakness and point to individuals who violated them while still becoming successful. Once we've established a humanistic definition of success, I believe I can provide more names of individuals who leveraged these honorable personality traits and behaviors to benefit their fellow man rather than those who blatantly disregarded them. How much greater good could've been accomplished by a deeply flawed genius if they'd been more principled? You've seen enough adventure and superhero movies to accept the premise that King Arthur in *Camelot* finally came to understand, that "might for right" is the moral high ground.[4]

As mentioned earlier, some of these principles may not be new to you. However, if you're like me, understanding or recalling a couple of essential concepts and then adopting them can make a big difference. By the way, I did learn a few of these principles in school, it just took being on the job for me to make the association. My genuine hope is that what follows will allow you to accelerate your accumulation of insight and knowledge so you can then apply it. Success and best wishes to you in your personal lives and in your careers! As one man I worked closely with for years put it, "Why not you?"

---

[4] "*Camelot* (1967): Quotes." *IMDb*, 2023, imdb.com/title/tt0061439/quotes/?ref_=tt_trv_qu. Accessed 3 March 2023.

ANNOTATED TABLE OF CONTENTS

SECTION ONE: CAREER NAVIGATION

The Most Important Word 1
Why personal credibility is our most valuable asset

Planting Seeds 6
How to win acceptance of our worthwhile proposals

Earn More Than We're Paid 9
Being able to justify our compensation makes it easier to be generously rewarded

Avoid Openly Disagreeing with the Boss 12
Alternative exchanges that allow us to achieve win-win agreements with our supervisor

The Best Analysis Prevails 15
Why accurate data is such a vital element in making good decisions

Respond Quickly 17
The negative impact of not addressing problems or misconceptions in a timely manner

Overwhelming To-Do Lists 20
An effective approach to relieve anxiety while fulfilling our duties

Chip on Our Shoulder?..22
How being defensive leads to performance failure

Become the Go-To Person..26
Gaining our team's confidence while successfully leading them

Over Prepared...29
Being primed for opportunities versus the consequences of being underprepared

Always Give Our Best...33
The benefits of offering full effort even when things aren't going our way

Influencing Impressions 37
Understanding how to create positive impressions and avoid negative reactions

Was it the Assignment Given?..42
The value of clarifying a task and carrying it out to our boss's satisfaction

Clarify Without Displaying Ignorance.......................................44
How to acquire more information without embarrassing ourselves

Seek and Apply Advice...45
Shunning feedback eventually results in undesirable outcomes

Paying Your Dues 48
What you can expect to encounter your first few years on the job

Big Fish, Little Pond 51
Why employment by a small firm can provide good opportunities

Find a Mentor..52
A mentor is often in the best position to help us get ahead

What Potential Employers Seek 55
Nine characteristics desired by most employers

Interview When Invited 56
How to keep employment options open, without damaging relationships

SECTION TWO: LEADERSHIP & MANAGEMENT

Would You Follow Someone Like Yourself? 59
Perform a self-assessment to determine if your managerial style is inspiring and principled

Handling a Crisis 62
Enact planned steps in sequence when facing emergencies

Reports can Mislead 65
Overdependence on reports doesn't replace inspecting conditions in person

Control the Situation 67
Handling insubordinate behavior without worsening the circumstances

Two Strikes Allowed 72
Why this rule establishes fair expectations among everyone

Identify and Monitor Pulse Points 73
Employ a transparent, systemic method of monitoring all key indicators

Controlling and Utilizing Overtime 77
Practical tips on how to minimize overtime and when to employ it

Order Serves Success 84
Organization and simplicity save valuable resources

Research Reoccurring Problems to the Individual 87
Blaming the group for an individual's repeated failures is a surefire method to kill morale

Why Create a Report? 88
How the introduction of a report solves some performance failures

Micromanage Non-Performers 90
Why focusing attention on unmotivated employees ultimately benefits the rest of the department

Everyone Doing Their Share 93
Our team expects us to ensure everyone is carrying their fair share of the load

Establishing Accountability 96
Enforce standards and consequences while tactfully communicating with only the offenders

Meet Regularly with Direct Reports 100
The benefits of planned one-on-one meetings to discuss vital topics

SECTION THREE: MOTIVATION

Failing Takes Energy 103
Winning takes less additional time than you might think

One Team 104
When everyone is focused on the same outcome, we'll foster good results

Ask, Don't Command 109
We don't need to be abrasive to get team members to follow directions

Walking the Walk 109
Illustrations of leading by example

Set Higher Standards 111
The power of striving for excellence

Genuine Concern and Frequent Appreciation 115
The symbiotic consequences of caring for our coworkers and recognizing their efforts

Three Types of Workers 118
How each group approaches work

What About Your Motivation? 120
Understanding some theories of motivation and their personal impact

SECTION FOUR: RELATIONSHIPS

The Blame Game 125
Minimize the harmful effects when others make unfounded accusations

The Power of Relationships 127
Illustrations of how associations can boost our career

Love the One We're With 129
Why and how to be loyal to our current employer

Employment is a Two-Way Street 131
Few employees consider matters from their supervisor's perspective

Smile and be Approachable 133
Take down barriers and enjoy interacting with all people

Our Own Worst Enemy 135
Avoid behaviors that ostracize us from our coworkers

Seek Respect Before Friendship 138
Friendship can be a byproduct of being a conscientious team member

Why Apologize? 140
Supervisors earn more respect if they don't pretend to be perfect

Create Bridges, Not Enemies 142
Enemies are an energy black hole, so work with others even if they're difficult

Don't Turn a Positive into a Negative 145
Our inclination to be critical can ruin or prevent efforts that should be celebrated

Taking Care of Customers 147
Know who our customers are and how to prevent them from becoming upset

SECTION FIVE: ETHICS

Spend Goodwill, but Carefully 151
Exercise prudence before and after receiving a favor

Willing to Forgive 154
Appreciate what others do for us rather than expecting them to fill our every need

Take the High Road 155
Doing the right things for the right reason is the best approach

Squeaky Clean 157
Never give anyone a reason to reprimand or fire you by violating rules

Give the Credit to the Team 160
Praise the team for their contributions and our superiors will recognize the good coaching

Good Humor Only..162
The workplace has no place for derogatory or off-color joking

A Short Harassment Policy 164
Keep it clear and simple and know how to enforce the rule

SECTION SIX: ODDS & ENDS

Multi-Tasking: Virtue or Vice?...167
When multi-tasking should and shouldn't be employed

When and How to Negotiate 169
Understanding the timing and approaches to improve our compensation package

Which Communications to Return 174
Identifying the messages to which we should and shouldn't respond

Time Off 174
Guidelines for managing our time off and requests from the team

Handling Life's Stresses... 177
Straight forward coping mechanisms for relieving pressure

Maintain Balance..178
How to decide which conflicting concerns must be given our attention

SECTION ONE

CAREER NAVIGATION

THE MOST IMPORTANT WORD

If I could teach aspiring managers only one concept, without question I would pick accumulating personal credibility. This principle was taught to me by a peer at one firm who then hired me to work for him at another. Though we occasionally didn't agree, I consider him to have been my most important mentor and a dear friend.

Credibility is the most important thing we can possess as a manager. It pertains equally to our relationships with those above us in the chain of command, our dealings with peers, and our interactions with those who work under our direction. If we don't have it, we'll find it very difficult to achieve anything of good consequence.

Credibility is something we earn. How? It's amassed by successfully accomplishing tasks we're assigned or which we volunteer to perform. Credibility is also attained by taking the initiative to correct problems and make improvements (see: "Respond Quickly" and "Was it the Assignment Given?"). This transpires on the job, but it also accrues as we go about undertaking to do good as a member of humanity. This trustworthiness increases by not only conducting ourselves competently, but with as much compassion as reasonably possible.

This integrity is so important that one should go to great lengths to never go on record with lies or inaccurate facts. Have information, like sales results or production metrics, in hand even if you must carry a cheat sheet. Responding to questions that we're expected to know aids in demonstrating our capability to others. On the other hand, not knowing the details or making bad guesses will quickly get a person labeled incompetent. Should we ever find that we've misconstrued facts and then passed them on, we should retrace our steps as swiftly as possible back to our boss, peer, or subordinate. Retract incorrect data by sharing accurate material and refreshing their memories as to the original context, if necessary. Although this can be a bit embarrassing, it's far wiser than having someone else get to them with the truth of the matter (intentionally or not) and by so doing discredit us. Likewise, if we've done something wrong or made a mistake that will influence the efforts of the team, tell the truth (see: "Why Apologize?"). This is a healthier alternative than having others expose our mistake since we haven't added deceit to the equation.

The first time I was aware of violating this principle occurred while I was director of distribution, reporting to the mentor mentioned previously, at a large warehouse operation. It consisted of 600,000 square feet of space, including several satellite locations. We'd just completed a multimillion-dollar project to update almost the entire material handling system inside the primary facility. Of course, after spending this much money senior management hoped the enhancements would meet all expectations with regard to service improvement and return on investment. There was also an unspoken expectation that we wouldn't need to make any other capital improvement expenditures for a respectable amount of time.

It was in these circumstances that I requested twenty heavy-duty merchandise carts, which would cost about twenty thousand dollars today. Not a relatively large amount but unplanned, so it wouldn't go unnoticed on the monthly budget recap or might require a separate capital request application. One of my managers had assured me he needed them to better facilitate the flow of bulky merchandise that couldn't travel the conveyor system through the main facility. Priding myself on getting the necessary resources for my staff as speedily as possible when there was a legitimate need, a verbal request was made to my boss. I trusted in the mantra, "If you want them to get their job done, either get them the necessary tools or explain why they're not forthcoming" (see: "Become the Go-To Person"). The concept of how these carts would be used made sense to me and the requesting manager assured me the need was real.

Well, you probably guessed it: about two weeks after the carts were delivered; my boss was doing a walkthrough and saw virtually all of them sitting empty. Clearly, they weren't being utilized in any degree close to what I'd indicated in my sales pitch. The staff hadn't been trained on how to put them to use.

He tactfully confronted me with that fact and reminded me that I rather passionately assured him how badly we needed this equipment, that the money would be spent wisely, and that they would save us labor dollars. Instead, they were just collecting dust. The next time I said I needed tools and wanted to spend limited budget money, he indicated he might require me to write an analysis so he could confirm I had the facts right.

That's the stuff of which credibility is made. Not only did my integrity take a hit, but so did the requesting manager's. I'd been in the enviable position of simply asking my boss for resources or support, and he'd give them readily. Now I was going to have to go to the effort of writing a thorough report, with the return on investment (ROI) spelled out and the possibility I still might not get my request granted.

Fact finding should always occur, but not having to turn research into a polished report and wait for a thorough review because I wasn't completely trusted would obviously save time. There are some settings where writing business case analyses to justify resource acquisitions is normal, but my point is that you need to monitor your standing in terms of normal practices. Do we have to jump through hoops not required of others? Why?

It doesn't matter if we're given an assignment or if we volunteer, we must successfully meet expectations and deadlines. A competent boss will be quick to support our efforts if in return results are delivered that positively reflect on the team as well. If you fail to hit commitments, or if like me you're given assets that you don't use, you may find that your boss will need to go to additional lengths so that their trustworthiness isn't damaged along with that of the team. After all, they're the coach, and they're expected to deliver in the same manner.

Another tip relates to how we respond to what seems an innocent or merely inconsequential inquiry. We should support our supervisor in any endeavor that isn't counterproductive or immoral. The same boss from the previous example got frustrated with how I responded to questions when the owners of the business came and walked through our part of the organization. The CEO or president would typically ask me, "How are you doing?" My response was usually something short like, "Fine, thanks for asking." Afterward, my boss would be justifiably upset. He'd spent valuable time covering strategic or tactical needs and initiatives with these executives (see: "Planting Seeds"). Then, when one of the owners approached me to validate an issue, I in effect contradicted what my supervisor had conveyed by telling them everything was good. Obviously, at this stage in my career, I wasn't astute enough to understand the implications of a simple interaction. He strongly suggested, "When they ask you if everything is okay, say something like, 'Personally, I'm fine, but we do have several challenges that I'd like to discuss with you.'" With this approach, I wouldn't come across as unsociable or negatively impact my boss's ability to champion our needs, but rather assist the effort.

Quite a few years earlier, I left my role as a store manager in a high-fashion retailer to join a specialty chain. My job was assistant store manager in a very well-run 60,000 square foot unit where I was tutored by my boss, the store manager. He'd been on vacation for a few days when the vice president of stores came through on short notice to do a walkthrough (which was only slightly better than no notice). The vice president had a reputation as a stickler for the smallest details, which wasn't necessarily a derogatory portrayal in this work culture. Were the edges on the fixtures exactly one inch from the aisles? Were all display fixtures and shelves completely full of merchandise? Was every single shirt or blouse, including the one just handled and inspected by a customer, neatly folded? Had all glass been cleaned of fingerprints and was every surface wiped off or dusted? Another example of this high standard was that a customer should be able to walk up to a fixture displaying only one style of men's golf shirts and find it sorted perfectly by color and then size. Being "in standard" was easily monitored since each size of shirt was progressively bigger in the shoulders and longer in length. This creates a uniform pattern when looking at the tails of the shirts because the larger sizes hang closer to the ground.

The executive stayed for about an hour. He must have had some feeling that I was getting a little full of myself, because he hadn't yet found anything to call out. Nevertheless, he wasn't about to give up. As I walked him out to his car, we entered the vestibule at the south customer entry to the store. He looked up and undoubtedly to his pleasure saw some rust on the sprinkler head above us. For a couple of minutes, he dressed me down for this infraction to make certain there wasn't any excessive air left in my ego. Remember, loose ends are a drain on a good reputation, so try to always make sure the entire assignment is completed. Despite the fact he'd found something to fault (thankfully, it was quite small), soon thereafter I was offered my own store assignment. This was thanks in great part to the store team who functioned at a very high standard and created credibility that I could share in.

May I make a few suggestions? First, don't generously pad timelines since someone will come along and perform the task faster. Do include some reasonable allowances for the unforeseen so that you under-promise, slightly, and then over-deliver. Second, avoid telling just your side of the story. Try to provide an objective representation of all issues. Your boss will hear the other side and wonder why you didn't share all the facts. Third, do everything possible to not make the same mistake twice. Finally, count on others to protect your integrity and communicate that quid pro quo expectation as necessary. For instance, if a vendor acknowledges they're giving you their best price your boss shouldn't be able to call them up and get a better deal.

If you don't have an extremely good grasp on where you stand (many don't), I strongly encourage you to assess if you have credibility with your peers. There are numerous ways to go about this and I'll offer one: ask to join a temporary task force or team by inquiring if you can assist them with any projects that involve shared responsibilities. If they welcome your partnership or involvement, that indicates you have some measure of reliability. They'll already have opinions as to whether you're well informed and if they see you as a catalyst or an obstacle for getting things done correctly and on schedule. See if your colleagues listen to your thoughtful input (don't just fabricate meaningless ideas or facts) or are willing to implement actions you've recommended. If you're well-received, you've apparently shown previously that you're also committed to the team's success. If your standing is that you focus on irrelevant or counterproductive efforts, don't do your homework, or fail to make good things happen, others will be slow to partner or engage with you. After all, they don't want you to damage their reputation. *Warning: Don't blow a bit of positive feedback out of proportion. Just because you have a little credibility with a few people doesn't mean you even remotely possess as much as you need with everyone else with whom you work closely.*

PLANTING SEEDS

Learn the value of introducing proposals over time using masterful technique. This might begin with a simple comment mentioning the benefits of a change to the current course of action and then expand from there. Complement the effort with impeccable timing in introducing and gaining acceptance of your thoroughly scrutinized ideas and suggestions. Deliver the message when the listener isn't rushed or in an emotionally charged state. I recall how some mornings one team member monitoring the employee entrance prior to store hours would corner me as I walked in. Although I tried to be responsive, I wanted to turn around and go home if this was what the day held. Perhaps if he'd identified that I wasn't a morning person he might've chosen his timing with more care. For revolutionary ideas, after your team has worked through all the details and are united in their commitment to the new approach, consider going as a small group to your boss if circumstances warrant. It's a great form of subtle recognition for partners, and it's hard to say no to a committed team.

Don't unnerve your boss by dropping a crisis in their lap last-minute when you've had some warning yourself. We've all heard the adage, "no surprises." Another experience involved a manager coming to me one day and without warning saying she needed to hire two new employees. As I asked when, "Right now" was the response. This caught me off guard since there was only one other person in her department and the additional head count hadn't been budgeted. When we began to discuss the need, she said, "Well, I did mention this a few months ago." As I recalled, the conversation was more like, "I may need to hire a few people down the road." While this may have been a good start, it certainly doesn't constitute a thoughtful strategy for preparing your boss to support the hiring of more staff. What I'm saying is that we need to keep watering the seeds we plant frequently and monitor their growth. This allows the decision maker to consider the request in terms of circumstance and to hear others' support. It also allows them time to either do research on their own, including coming up with strategies to gain funding, or at least to keep an open mind when and if the concept comes up elsewhere. Anticipate the planting of these seeds so that the harvest (approval) coincides with the need.

This concept also relates closely to the saying, "the squeaky wheel gets the grease." If we've made a request for service from another department and it's gone past an acceptable amount of time, we can plant seeds of expectation by diplomatically inquiring at regular intervals regarding the status of our appeal. This helps emphasize the importance of the project and establishes that we won't accept inaction (see: "Seek Respect Before Friendship").

Sun Tzu offers in *The Art of War*, "everybody can see superficially how a battle is won; what they cannot see is the long series of plans and combinations which has preceded the battle."[5] Although working in the business world isn't war, understand that most decisions are determined before you go to meetings. One of my big oversights during the middle stage of my career was to introduce carefully researched but out-of-the-blue suggestions at gatherings with merchandise managers and other department heads. When it was my turn and I'd presented a well-studied and documented idea, one or more of the merchandise managers would say something like, "I don't want to do that." When asked why by a corporate executive, sometimes the reply was as pathetic as, "I don't know. I just don't feel like we should do it." This was quite a culture since you didn't even have to deal in facts—just emotions. The idea would then be tabled with the explanation that we needed a consensus (see: "Control the Situation"). My boss, who witnessed several of these failures, taught me to rally as much support as possible before the meeting. Engage everybody who you believe will support your proposal. Next, go in person to those who you think will object and try to win their cooperation as well. This may require some quid pro quo agreements. Then when you're in front of everyone, including the ranking leader, they'll be able to observe that nearly everyone supports the program. This may be enough to tip the scales in your favor over the objections of a dissenter or two, especially if they're not highly regarded.

---

[5] Tzu, Sun. *The Art of War*. Translated by Lionel Giles, 1910. *Project Gutenberg*. gutenberg.org/cache/epub/132/pg132-images.html. Accessed 3 March 2023.

CONCEPTS OF MANAGING

Related to this concept are two simple warnings. First, don't confuse managing your interactions with your superior (i.e., planting seeds) with manipulating them (see: "Take the High Road"). Your goal is to make your boss's job of decision making easier. Only sharing part of the facts will come back to haunt you. Second, if you gain approval to proceed with an initiative and things don't go as planned, deliver bad news in person. This permits you to respond to questions, assess how the message is perceived, provide clarification, obtain any direction, and most importantly to provide your well-conceived plan to correct the situation (see: "Become the Go-To Person").

EARN MORE THAN WE'RE PAID

In a recent *The Born Loser* comic strip by Art and Chip Sansom, the main character, Brutus Thornapple, approaches his boss, Rancid Veeblefester, and says, "Good news, chief! I have an idea…it could save thousands of dollars a year for the company, without reducing productivity." His boss replies, "Oh, you're tendering your resignation?"[6]

You've heard it before: we're either part of the problem or part of the solution. We must make ourselves valuable and difficult to replace (see: "Over Prepared"). If we want to be irreplaceable, we have to do our very best to make sure our contribution exceeds our pay by as much as possible. Seeking to understand what explicit impact our boss values regarding our efforts can be a part of the equation (see: "Seek and Apply Advice").

Once again, I reiterate: we should carry out the intent of our position which encompasses performing the job we've been hired to do and not just the portion of it we enjoy doing (see: "Avoid Openly Disagreeing with the Boss"). Don't offer a cursory effort at completing core duties while spending most of the time playing politics. This will eventually catch up

---

[6] Sansom, Chip and Art Sansom. *The Born Loser*. GoComics. 10 January 2023. gocomics.com/the-born-loser/2023/01/10. Accessed 27 Mary 2023.

with you. Take efforts to the next level and beyond. Be keenly aware of opportunities to either make more money for the firm or to eliminate waste. Success often follows a team's ability to foresee and implement bigger, important initiatives.

At one juncture, a quality assurance manager working in a distribution center failed to alert the staff that we had a product lot nearing its expiration date. He approved some capsules—with only nine months of shelf life left—to be placed into a merchandise kit whose components should have had 24 months before expiring. Because he failed to change the end date for this component in the warehouse management system, the newly assembled collection of products containing the capsules was received and handled in typical first in/first out (FIFO) fashion. The result was that the kit had to be pulled after only selling two-thirds of the lot's inventory because a customer called attention to the discrepancy.

Soon thereafter, the same manager submitted a material disposition form to write-off and dispose of that product contained within the collection (this didn't include the labor costs to extract and replace the capsules). He then said to one of the executives, "I could buy a new car with what's getting wasted." The senior manager was rightfully upset, but the source of the failure wasn't immediately apparent since the QA manager placed the blame elsewhere. It took a while, but eventually it came to light that his failure was the cause of the waste. Within about a year, other performance failures resulted in his termination because he was costing the company much more than he was being paid.

Be willing to prove yourself. Usually, no one owes us anything. I took a significant pay cut to accept what eventually became my best paying job. It took several years to get back to the wage of my previous employment, but I then made up the income difference over the next few years. Strap on your helmet every day trying to make the firm better. In time, the return on your effort should become obvious.

During that same period, I periodically interacted with a couple of employees who both received very good paychecks. Honestly, I couldn't see what they were doing to earn their salaries and I attempted to tactfully raise the matter with their bosses. Both were eventually let go, but not before they'd received hundreds of thousands of dollars in wasted wages over their tenure. One had worked at the company for seven or eight years. He made in the neighborhood of six figures, but it would be difficult to enumerate any notable accomplishments from him over that period. He maintained some relationships with organizations or individuals outside of the company, he produced a couple of rather simple monthly reports, and he sat on a few committees and offered his opinions.

Have you ever heard this story of the young farm hand? As was custom in England, he attended a fair where he could wait to be hired by local farmers. A well-known farmer approached him and asked what he could do and the young man answered, "I can sleep on a windy night." After answering several other questions and repeating his answer, the farmer was intrigued by the young man's character and hired him all the while seeing no value in the farm hand's proffered skill. The young man knew more about his future boss than expected, and was aware that his farm lay near a coast where frequent storms occurred. Soon after he began working, a terrible windstorm arose and the farmer urgently went and called for the young farm hand to wake up. When the farmer got no response, he went and checked on the animals and farmstead himself and found everything sound, secured, and safe. It was only then that he realized what the young farm hand had meant: "Ah…I see now how it's the lad can sleep. He leaves nothing to be done which ought to be done and can be done before he goes to bed; therefore, when he gets there, he has nothing to do but sleep."[7]

I first applied this lesson while working at a home store for a large department store retailer, and scored some real points with my boss prior to taking a one-week vacation. I accomplished this by simply creating a

---

[7] Whittaker, Thomas. "How to Sleep on a Windy Night." *Brighter England and the Way to It*. Hodder and Stoughton, 1891. pp. 259-261.

packet of easy-to-follow daily instructions listing the tasks (ad set-ups, merchandise transfers, floor display changes, etc.) that needed to be completed and who had been asked to fulfill them in my absence.

You don't want to be in a situation where you can't justify your compensation. Perform a self-analytical litmus test. Ask if you're worth what the company has paid you—including benefits—over your period of employment. Have you saved or generated more profit than what the company has compensated you over your tenure period? Is it something you can calculate and defend on your resume? Even better, can you refer to monthly reports where your value is documented in dollars and cents? If you can't justify your payroll expense, then you may be expendable. Just like baseball players who have their salaries weighed against the composite value of indicators like batting averages, runs batted in, runs scored, or fielding percentages, look at your overall impact. Your contribution can be measured in sales created, expenses controlled or minimized, inventory protected, turnover reduced, or new processes implemented, to suggest just a few.

Finally, one of the greatest ways to help earn more for the company is to not only develop the ability to accomplish this ourselves, but to also be the catalyst to get coworkers to engage in this endeavor. Superiors want someone who can lead out in achieving what is in the best interest of the firm.

AVOID OPENLY DISAGREEING WITH THE BOSS

The district manager at one of my retail employers held weekly conference calls with his store managers. Among other things, part of the purpose for this call was to convey merchandising directives to support upcoming sales events, seasonal changes, and the like. One charismatic store manager was christened the "Man of Steel and Velvet" because it was as though he possessed a firm hand in a very soft glove. The perception was that he had a favored status with our boss and other upper management team members. I'm sure the fact that he looked like Tom Selleck didn't hurt. He was always agreeable. Senior executives loved him because he was like the guy on a high school sports team that would say, "Just give me his number, coach, and I won't let him score again" (see: "Become the Go-To Person").

Some of the instructions in these calls occasionally required a lot of extra effort for what seemed to be little benefit or return. During one call, I remember voicing concerns and sought an exception to one elaborate undertaking the merchant group expected us to carry out. The messenger—my supervisor—heard me out, but an exemption wasn't forthcoming. Later, when visiting the store of "Mr. Charismatic," I noted that he hadn't made the required modification for which I'd sought an exception. I'd just completed the not-so-insignificant transformation the day before. I asked why he hadn't complied and was told he got approval from the district manager: "I just called him up after the conference call and asked if he would have a problem if I did it a bit differently, and he said okay." At that point, the rest of us had been stressing over how we were going to accomplish the formidable task, yet it was already in the "Chosen One's" rearview mirror. He'd gained the necessary allowance, making the undertaking much easier to complete.

It was then that the light finally went on for me: he was simply being respectful. Requesting a generous exception in front of all of my peers put my boss in a bit of a squeeze. The spotlight was directly on him to see how he would handle my request for a concession, with all of his other store managers waiting for him to start distributing "Get Out of Jail Free" cards. That wasn't the right time to buck the system. Like the "Man of Steel and Velvet," I needed to seek my immunity privately.

When your manager is conducting a meeting or conference call and presents an idea or goal, they're looking for commitment to tackle the task. If you start listing all of the reasons why it won't work or argue unimportant details, your boss will see your effort as adversarial. You become a roadblock preventing everyone in the group from moving forward (see: "Chip on Our Shoulder?"). If you have a small concern or issue you want heard, save it for a personal moment later. Seek out your supervisor afterward and say, "Would you make this small allowance?" It will often be granted, and they won't feel like you're trying to derail everyone from accomplishing the essence of the job. If you can't keep a lid on your emotions until a better time, don't say much more than, "There is a small issue I want to run by you later."

While it may make you feel smart to correct or challenge your boss when their director is present, how intelligent is that, really? This also applies to contradicting your manager in emails or side conversations. Over the years, I've witnessed this behavior many times: some subordinate finds it necessary to point out a small, unimportant variation in the facts. Once, a team member argued that the increase was "actually 21.8%" after their manager went on record that sales were up a bit over 20%. This is obviously a poor attempt to show a supervisor's boss how bright they are, but it only makes them appear immature.

If it's a serious matter, you can still honor some of the basic principles found in *Crucial Conversations*[8] by discussing your concerns with the leader privately. If it's a very grave matter personally or professionally and you still can't come to terms, ask them to accompany you so you can discuss the matter further up the chain of command (see: "Two Strikes Allowed" and "Planting Seeds"). Pick your battles when you refuse to suffer in silence. In doing so, remember to be diplomatic, to avoid making it personal (you just have differing views), and to pay attention to time and place which are very important to the outcome (see: "Clarify Without Displaying Ignorance").

This advice isn't intended to prevent you from asking higher-ups for resources when they're justified, just do so respectfully and in a cause-and-effect context. When I was starting high school, one summer I worked

---

[8] Grenny, Joseph et al. *Crucial Conversations: Tools for Talking When Stakes are High*, 3rd edition. McGraw Hill, 2021.

with a friend at a cannery. For part of the season, we were assigned to unload flatbed trailers of cherries pulled by tractors. The fruit, harvested into crates, came from nearby orchards. It was much more efficient as a two-man job, each of us grabbing one side of the crate and dumping the contents into a capture tank where the cherries were rinsed off with water before being conveyed into the plant for processing. Sometimes we worked 14-hour days (so much for youth labor laws). Early one afternoon, I became extremely nauseated and went home, where I threw up multiples times and then lay down for about two hours. When I awoke, I felt like I needed to go back and finish the shift. When I arrived, I was surprised to learn my buddy had been unloading the trailers by himself. Only occasionally would one of the farmers help, since this was their only break and part of the service the cannery was supposed to provide. Immediately, I reiterated how genuinely ill I'd been. He was unsympathetic and responded that he would rather have been sick than stuck doing the job alone. I felt badly and wished he'd asked for help, but like me, he was too young to assess the situation and conclude they certainly weren't going to fire him for asking.

THE BEST ANALYSIS PREVAILS

When faced with difficult decisions, painstakingly analyze the situation. Do your homework and be careful not to understate or overstate the impact of pertinent conditions. This includes researching possible consequences and deciding if the department, division, and company can live with them. Preparing for the worst is the most important part, since it's usually a pretty good guarantee things will never be quite that bad. This advice applies to winning approval of your proposals over other options (see: "Planting Seeds"). If you've thought everything through and carefully documented such things as existing circumstances, ROI, successful application of the approach elsewhere, and contingency plans, you'll usually carry the day and experience successful implementation even when there were preliminary objections.

When you find yourself in a situation where your team's plan will be compared to other possible solutions, this advice is even more pertinent. Don't rely on good fortune to sway in your favor. Earn the support and approval you seek by doing the best job you can analyzing the circumstances and developing the most thorough and thoughtful program for successful implementation.

Along these lines, one of my biggest regrets was not doing a better job researching details more thoroughly before making decisions, especially during my early career. Hoping they could learn from my mistakes, I advised my children to perform indispensable groundwork prior to picking a major or pursuing a profession. This included the counsel, "Before you choose a job, spend time talking to professionals in that field and ask about their workday. What are the critical skills they must possess? What is the downside to making your living that way? Is that really what you want to do every day for the rest of your working life?"

My two sons became attorneys (very handy if I ever need to post bail). A brother, brother-in-law, nephew, daughter-in-law, and a cousin are also lawyers. One of my sons worked for my lawyer brother while he was attending law school. It would have been a real oversight for my boys not to talk to relatives about the type of law they practiced and to ask questions. Don't let life take you somewhere you're not prepared or don't want to go, purely because you neglected to research and plan. You'll have much less aggravation and enjoy your life a lot more. Even if you're further down life's trail, there are options and opportunities to improve your situation if you're willing to invest some effort. As Thich Nhat Hanh counsels, "Many of us slog through life without conscious awareness or intention. We set ourselves a course and we barrel ahead, without stopping to ask whether this path is fulfilling our most important goals."[9]

---

[9] Hanh, Thich Nhat. *No Mud, No Lotus*. Parallax Press, 2014. p. 36.

Another area meriting your effort includes interview preparation. This is embarrassing, but I'll tell it anyway: while interviewing for a job with the owner and top executives of a firm, I unknowingly twice used a business term that was considered outdated and uncomplimentary of the industry. The second time, the president almost stood up out of his chair to correct me. The miracle is that I got the job, despite being a dunce.

RESPOND QUICKLY

Every moment we delay in responding to challenges or criticism—whether valid or the result of misconception—allows political winds to fan the fire. If we don't solve the difficulty or reply rapidly enough, a small brush fire can grow into a firestorm. If there was a performance failure, acknowledge the problem and share the steps that are being taken to prevent it from happening again. The worst thing we can be accused of is allowing failure to happen. We also can't afford to be accused of being unresponsive. If upper management wants an issue to go away, they'll allow us the opportunity to fix it. If we have a reputation for rectifying difficulties, they'll want us to continue these efforts.

When resolutions aren't suitable, something like the original problem will occur again. We must learn the lesson or repeatedly face the consequences of our mistakes. Upper management—with a memory like an elephant—will remember that this breakdown happened before, and they'll also recall that we said we knew how to fix it. Wanting to avoid a reoccurrence, they'll start looking around for someone else who can generate the solution. If this gets to be a pattern, they may look to replace us.

Although the following episode didn't involve a terminable offense, it does provide a simple case study. A purchasing agent once accidentally ordered ten times as much of a publication as needed because he hadn't questioned a math error in the system-generated forecast (see: "Reports can

Mislead"). When I learned of the dollar amount of the expense—which might end up being discussed at a water cooler—I asked his supervisor to get involved. They were encouraged to approach our exceptional vendor, explain the situation, and request that we only pay for the overage at their cost, without the normal markup. Because of the vendor's long-game perspective they discounted both labor and materials. An email was sent out explaining how the error was handled. This was the last we heard of it. It also confirmed that we had a vendor who was a true business partner and we made them aware we wanted to return the favor. Like the old fable about how gossip is like spreading feathers, we couldn't pick all the feathers up, but we got enough of them that the threat to our reputation had been defused (see: "The Most Important Word").

If we don't have all of the facts at hand, we still need to let the interested parties know that we're on top of the research but that it will take time. When that information is gathered, inform them in an expedient manner. If employing the solution falls within our authority, implement it as soon as possible. If approval is required, document a request swiftly so any lag time won't be attributed to our inattention. Send timely follow-up requests as fitting. Then, put the corrective plan into action as soon as approval occurs.

Let me share an example that illustrates the type of hurdles that can be encountered. A senior manager, from another functional area, expressed doubts that members of one of the purchasing departments I'd been responsible for were good negotiators. Based on the education, specialized training, and experience of that staff, I disagreed with her assessment. Rather than fruitlessly argue, I adopted the team's earlier recommendation to bring in a top-notch consultant with Fortune 500 credentials to help train the group. This would hopefully put criticism to rest, especially with any members of the executive team. Having the consultant would be worthwhile in several ways since they could speak to our strengths and help us eliminate any weaknesses they discovered.

Even though he was consistently working long hours, the assignment to locate such an expert was given to an assistant manager, in part because he'd recently shared his desire to advance (see: "Overwhelming To-Do Lists"). One consultant was identified, but we didn't have a very good handle on his credentials, and we hadn't explored other avenues to identify additional candidates. Because the project languished, I found it necessary to go back and try to breathe some life into this effort by repeatedly asking for a status update, re-explaining the urgency and intent, and suggesting some ways to proceed. During this process, I couldn't help but think about the challenge promoting this assistant manager would present if something happened to the existing manager. He was a terrific person and a hard worker, but at this stage of his career would he be able to juggle more tasks without some falling through the cracks (see: "Over Prepared" and "Multi-Tasking: Virtue or Vice?")? The department manager and I continued our involvement until the effort was completed.

Success is composed of hard work and many mundane tasks, just like placing bricks in a wall (sorry, Pink Floyd). If you don't treat the placement of each one as important, and urgent when applicable, then the raising of the wall doesn't happen in a timely manner (I know because as a teenager I was a hod carrier for two bricklayers, which meant keeping them supplied in mortar and bricks). Little tasks and acts are part of the foundation upon which a successful venture is built. When we have minor projects, we should prioritize them but also treat them with proper resolve. Our boss doesn't want to have to complete our assigned tasks as well as their own. How we develop reliability will factor in when leadership decides if we're capable of more responsibility (see: "The Most Important Word").

As mentioned earlier, when we're promoted we have a responsibility to do our entire job and not just what we deem important (see: "Was it the Assignment Given?" and "Always Give Our Best"). Our superiors watch us to determine if we're handling our assignment and successful taking our part of the organization forward. Do we work well with the team and keep them on task? Do we accomplish the goals we've been given? Does upper management say to themselves, "They have things under control and there's another area they might effectively oversee," so leadership is inclined to give us more tasks? If we're carrying out our duties, then we shouldn't wait to volunteer when an opportunity presents itself (see: "Over Prepared"). This action indicates that we have additional bandwidth. Yes, we may be at our comfort level, but if we want to get ahead, we need to demonstrate we possess additional capacity and can manage more challenges with a capable team.

In another *The Born Loser* comic, Brutus is confronted by his boss about an assignment: "You don't have it ready, yet? When I say I want it now, I mean now!" After his boss leaves, Brutus turns to the reader and says, "The chief is a now or never kind of guy…unfortunately, I'm more of a sooner or later guy."[10] Quite simply, our sense of urgency should exceed that of our boss. If it doesn't, we'll always be turning in assignments slower than they like. How would you feel about someone reporting to you that completes projects too slowly, especially if you had to follow up with them on a frequent basis? Put the shoe on the other foot (see: "Would You Follow Someone like Yourself?"). This includes reporting back when you've partially or fully completed an essential task without your supervisor having to ask. Return and report, whether face-to-face, in a text, email, voice message, or even on a Post-It note (see: "Was it the Assignment Given?").

OVERWHELMING TO-DO LISTS

There's an old saying, "When you're up to your neck in alligators it's easy to forget your initial objective was to drain the swamp."[11] The simple antidote

---

[10] Sansom, Chip and Art Sansom. *The Born Loser. GoComics*. 19 October 2022. gocomics.com/the-born-loser/2022/10/19. Accessed 11 April 2023.

[11] Quoted in Patterson, Margaret Jones and Robert H. Russell. *Behind the Lines: Case Studies in Investigative Reporting*. Columbia University Press, 1986. p. 203.

to this predicament is to go to your boss before you start to drown. Don't wait until you're near or have passed deadlines, because you've now made it harder to get help. Say to your supervisor, "I've determined I'm not going to be able to accomplish everything I've been assigned in a timely manner. It's not that I'm forgetting all of my duties; in fact, I maintain a list of all of my assignments. Would you be willing to sit with me and help me reprioritize these tasks, so I meet your expectations?"

When I've done this, I've found my superiors to be very helpful and interested. They were willing to tell me what they needed soon and what could go to the back burner for the time being. After all, there are some projects more urgent or important than others. Often, a couple of tasks are no longer even necessary. This alone makes the exercise worthwhile. You're giving the boss exactly what they want in the sequence they want it. They're also aware that you haven't overlooked projects that are important to them. They realize you pay attention and are conscientious. You buy yourself some time and take a lot of self-imposed pressure off, caused by working on less critical tasks out of sequence. On the off chance that your manager wants or needs it all now, take the opportunity to outline any additional means you'll need to hit the mark.

In a related vein, we may have supplemental resources available that we haven't realized. As a store manager, I would periodically check with an operations manager to review the status of jobs delegated to her. Occasionally, I would get either a non-verbal clue or response indicating she was buried or overwhelmed. Trying to help her manage that amount of work, I tried to coach with, "Just because I gave you those tasks, doesn't mean you need to do all of them yourself. You have a lot of people who work for you, and some of them would love something challenging to do when the store traffic is light."

When you have a workforce under your direction, delegation can help you manage your workload while providing them with development opportunities. As a young department manager in a furniture and appliance store, I learned this lesson upon encountering an older assistant store manager. He was a master of deputizing team members to complete projects. Prior to the advent of email, when mail and intercompany deliveries arrived he'd walk around the sales floor and assign associated tasks to the store staff. This would usually only take fifteen or twenty minutes. He trained most of the commissioned salespeople to do different parts of his paperwork. After watching this for a few days, I concluded they didn't mind the assignments because periods existed throughout the week when it was relatively quiet and these tasks helped them kill boredom while waiting for customers. The point is, duties that burden or bore us may not be unpleasant to someone else who wants to learn, stay busy, or get some recognition for a job well done (see: "Over Prepared"). We don't need to apologize for delegating an assignment if it's a good match with the person completing it.

CHIP ON OUR SHOULDER?

Try very hard to avoid being defensive. Instead, focus on solving the problem. An excuse-maker wears on the patience of upper management because they're a barrier to progress and improvement. Several experiences come to mind.

While working at a large retailer in the Intermountain West, we fielded a complaint that a couple of our largest and most expensive televisions (as opposed to modern flat screens) sent from the distribution center via tractor-trailer equipment to the stores, arrived with broken picture tubes. When I shared this complaint with the shipping manager, he immediately became defensive. His response was, "That can't be happening. We secure them to the vertical tie down track on the side of the trailer and put padded blankets over them." He also insinuated that the store's receiving personnel might be making up the problem.

Before we could address the difficulty, I now also had to expend extra effort convincing a member of my supervisory group that there was indeed a problem. I had to sit down with him a few hours later and counsel, "You need to keep an open mind about this. Do you think the receiving staff is making this up? It's almost a guarantee they're not unloading these TVs and then taking a hammer to the screens so they can make you—a person they've never met—look bad. Why would they do that? Reporting the problem and returning the broken sets back to the distribution center adds to their workload. You need to accept the fact that there's a real issue which needs to be addressed." *Note: In some instances, there are so many facts available that common sense can ascertain the truth. However, be careful not to jump to conclusions or overlook the need to investigate when the situation isn't crystal clear.*

This same individual, whom I did like, was later approached regarding the productivity of his staff loading outbound trailers. They were on an incentive plan and due to the lack of technology that existed, staff members had to separately report how many cartons or pallets they'd handled. Each material handler was assigned a set of trailers or doors and would manage the simultaneous loading of three to five trailers, depending on the sales volume of every store. However, they were supposed to help the person working adjacent to them if their workload was light. This concern about productivity came up when some members of the department were reporting a very high carton count handled—earning them a bonus—but the outbound carton numbers we collected from the entire processing area didn't support it. Their performance should have left them with fewer backlogs than other loaders, but instead we found their primary conveyor chutes were generally backed up. Other coworkers handling similar volume weren't making as much in bonus but were observed assisting other members of the team. We suspected that a couple of department employees were padding their numbers to get incentive pay they hadn't earned (see: "Reports can Mislead").

Once again, the aforementioned manager was resistant and defensive in response to these concerns. Because of this, my boss turned to the camera system to substantiate suspicions and overcome this man's unwavering viewpoint. *Note: I'm aware that experts don't recommend using the "eye in the sky" because it can demoralize staff and, in fact, that's what happened here.* The camera footage showed several of his loaders looking around to see if any supervision was present. They would then step into the trailer, out of camera view. Meanwhile, none of the cartons on the gravity feed conveyor were moving forward so it was obvious they weren't loading freight from the end of the chute. Five to twenty minutes later, the worker would come out of the trailer and start to push the cartons down the line again. This confirmed they were spending a considerable portion of their day unproductively.

When the shipping supervisor was confronted with this evidence, the facts were indisputable. He certainly felt embarrassed or, at the least, neglectful. The situation caught him off guard and he probably felt he'd lost too much credibility (see: "The Most Important Word"). He found a different job within three or four months, perhaps because it was such an arduous environment or maybe because he was ill at ease asking for assistance to correct their behavior. This was an unnecessary overreaction since the only corrective actions ever considered were for specific team members, certainly not him. Both my boss and I tried to offer our support. We tried to communicate that he hadn't created any of the problems and that they were just inherent to the work environment; more experienced managers encountered challenges like this as well. We felt he had a lot of potential and just needed not to take the observations personally and address these kinds of challenges with some rather straightforward remedies.

Earlier in my life, I experienced a dose of similar criticism which upset me as well. After the conclusion of a summer working on a pineapple plantation in Hawaii, two of our 18-year-old truck drivers complained to the owner of the youth employment agency about how we—the counselors (responsible for the conduct of the workforce and administering all non-work-related activity)—had failed to carry out our responsibilities. This was likely payback for refusing to allow them to go unescorted (per guidelines) into the nearby town whenever they wanted. A few weeks after we'd returned to the mainland, the head counselor I'd been paired with that summer refused to accept the invitation to sit with the owner and defend our actions. He was returning to college and decided to not sign up again for the following summer. As second-in-command and having shared living quarters with him, I was party to all of the major decisions made and accepted the summons.

We'd consulted by telephone regarding major decisions with our boss on at least a weekly basis while he directly administered the operation on another plantation that year. We'd gained his permission to proceed with critical actions like terminating a young man and sending him back home for possessing illegal drugs. Now the owner wanted to go over all of the details (which I later accepted he was entitled to do) associated with this complaint. At the time, I was anxious to defend myself and felt a bit frustrated for being second-guessed. Following our session, I worked another year for the pineapple plantations but as I relate elsewhere, when offered the head counselor position, I declined, hoping for that role elsewhere.

My advice regarding this subject is simple. First, consider the other person's position, especially if they're the owner, and respect their right to inquire and try to resolve problems. Listen to the issues, respond honestly, and be prepared to accept consequences.

Second, people we work with won't always like or agree with us. To deal with this when it arises, go out of your way to be as fair and prudent as possible in conduct and decision-making. This will allow you to defend—or at the very least, explain—actions, but more importantly, to live with yourself if an avalanche of criticism follows. Balance this with the philosophy to not be apologetic about a matter where you weren't involved and therefore have no culpability. Being conciliatory is one thing, but accepting responsibility if absolutely certain you had no fault is entirely another. We all have enough explaining to do without being a martyr for actions outside of our control.

BECOME THE GO-TO PERSON

Two relevant terms to this topic are "deal maker" and "deal breaker." In interacting with a third-party law firm representing my West Coast employer, I encountered an attorney who was so concerned with eliminating all risk that a major project was stalled almost two months trying to achieve this perfect state. A new facility we desperately needed was delayed, and I feared for my job. Having never been close to having a lawsuit filed or going to court over any contracts with which I'd been involved, I admit I was frustrated by the situation. I finally told this individual that I found it necessary to discuss the matter with their boss, but felt we both should go so all conditions were fairly discussed. Faced with that prospect, she decided the risk wasn't a big enough concern to prevent us from proceeding to execute the ancillary lease. By the way, the issue never surfaced because the condition truly didn't have any negative impact on the parties involved.

A man with whom I worked closely for years once told me, "Some people think coming to a meeting with an excuse is as good as getting the job done." It's our duty to accomplish assignments, fulfill responsibilities, and get our team the resources required so they can accomplish their mission. Don't shy away from this burden. We want to be seen as a person they can come to for answers and decisions. If we tell someone we'll do something to support their efforts, then we need to make it happen (see: "The Most Important Word").

If you need some time to accomplish the task, make certain to give those awaiting your actions a realistic timeframe, then beat it by a few days if possible. Similarly, if you're approached about a request with which you're not familiar or you feel unsure, explain that you need time to research the matter in greater depth (see: "Create Bridges, Not Enemies"). Don't feel pressured into making up a response on the spot to appear knowledgeable. After explaining why you've requested an accommodation to investigate, get back to them swiftly with the answer and reasoning. If it's something you know shouldn't or cannot be done, provide a clear explanation as to why not.

As this relates to overseeing a team, you don't want the staff to view you as an ineffective intermediary or senior management's messenger whom they must circumnavigate to get things done. *Warning: This doesn't mean we should pretend to be involved in decisions that are outside of our responsibilities or realm.*

Let's say a small receiving department requests powered equipment to move palletized freight from the dock area to the staging area for storage (sometimes called put-away), where a forklift then places the merchandise in the racking. It takes an average of four labor hours a day to move this freight with a manual pallet jack. If labor and benefits cost $30 an hour, you'll spend about $31,200 a year to perform this daily task. An electric riding pallet jack (called a walkie-rider) costs about $12,000 with tax and delivery. With it, they could move the same amount of freight in one hour a day for only $7,800 a year in labor to perform the job. When added to the cost of the new lift, the total is $19,800. Subsequently, the operation saves $11,400 a year in payroll and benefit expense making the return on your capital investment approximately 33 weeks or eight months. If that's an acceptable ROI at your firm, you need to tell your team you'll seek permission to proceed with the purchase. Once you've gained any necessary approvals, inform the department staff that the equipment has been ordered and when it will arrive (again, make sure you're reasonable with the projected arrival date to allow for any unanticipated delays).

On the other hand, perhaps eight months is an unacceptable ROI. As part of your due diligence, thoughtfully weigh any other relevant considerations. In this hypothetical instance, you can't present logic to your supervisor suggesting the purchase will improve safety, since no one has ever been injured moving freight from these trailers manually. Furthermore, there's no other application where the new electronic pallet jack could be used as backup equipment to support another process. At this point, you need to explain to the workforce that this acquisition doesn't currently meet the criteria established to safeguard your company's financial health.

If an individual is upset or struggling to understand the answer and your company has an open-door policy, offer to make an appointment for your employee with your boss that you'll also attend. By being present at the meeting, you'll eliminate future end-runs. It also preserves a healthy interactive environment and you can help ensure that the employee's perspective is reasonably expressed. Make sure your supervisor has all of the facts prior to the meeting. If during that appointment, the boss changes their mind (it happens) in support of the purchase, you helped facilitate that decision. It's a win-win. Walking out of the office you can say to your staff member, "You did a good job of presenting the request. We're going to get a new lift. Great. It will be helpful to have it." If your boss holds their ground, you can reinforce the decision and it subtly confirms with your employees that you were accurate in your initial assessment and response. It also lays the groundwork for handling upcoming requests, some of which may be approved. In this case, the equipment could get approved later on in a few months once receiving volume has increased to a point that satisfies your employer's desire for a six-month ROI.

OVER PREPARED

There's an old proverb, "Everything comes to him who hustles while he waits."[12] Welcome chances to learn a new skill, manage a different department, operate a new piece of equipment, or tackle another such opportunity. Invest your time and own money, if necessary, in continuing education. Become part of every worthwhile team venture you have the capacity to handle. My wife learned this lesson from her father. Before we were married, she worked at a bank and he advised her to "learn everything they're willing to teach you." This training might help you get a promotion or may be the difference in protecting you from a lay off. When things get tough or tight, your employer might keep you because you have multiple skills, allowing you to perform more than one role.

The actor Charles Grodin wrote, "Always, since earliest childhood, the message in my house was that to really achieve anything worthwhile takes a long time, and you have to work very hard to be good enough to achieve anything. That always made sense to me."[13] He later added, "I tried to make myself as good as possible, since it seemed to be the only thing in the whole profession over which I had any control.... I figured that with perseverance the opportunities would come. The question of how good I'd be when they did would determine my future."[14] It has also been written, "Experience is knowledge. Knowledge is confidence. Confidence is success."[15]

---

[12] Quoted in Jones, Francis Arthur. *Thomas Alva Edison: Sixty Years of an Inventor's Life*. Diamond Books, 1908, p. 14.

[13] Grodin, Charles. *It Would Be So Nice If You Weren't Here: My Journey Through Show Business*. William Morrow and Company, Inc. 1989. p. 74.

[14] Grodin, Charles. *It Would Be So Nice If You Weren't Here: My Journey Through Show Business*. William Morrow and Company, Inc. 1989. p. 106-107.

[15] @LifeBelowZeroTV. "Experience is knowledge. Knowledge is confidence. Confidence is success. And they all go together in that order. #LifeBelowZero." *Twitter*, 6 September 2017, 9:08 a.m., twitter.com/LifeBelowZeroTV/status/905447596201738240.

As parents, we advised our children to try to have a marketable skill when they exited college. My bachelor's degree was in Speech and Interpersonal Communication. Although I sincerely appreciated this training, I went back to graduate school because I didn't feel I was as employable as I wanted to be. People who have skills they can fall back on in tough times like tax preparation, teaching music lessons, welding, and operating heavy machinery (like my father) have my admiration and envy.

There may be times in life when you won't feel secure in a job despite all of your efforts to maintain a high standard of performance. Despite this condition, continue to learn as much as possible about anything that relates to your profession. Take comfort from the knowledge that even though this job may dry up and blow away or you can't get ahead with this leadership team in place, your skill set is current with best practices, and it's transferrable. This makes you employable with other firms in the market. If you feel uneasy about the pigeonhole you're in, start to actively broaden your abilities by taking any training—formal or informal—of which you can avail yourself. Volunteer for or pursue any assignments that expand the scope of your knowledge. Even if you don't get the first job you're shooting for, you'll be ready for other opportunities that will come your way (see: "Interview When Invited"). If you quit trying—which I see many workers do—it's very likely that you'll develop a negative attitude and bad work habits which will either prevent you from getting ahead in your current position or stop you from landing your dream job (see: "Our Own Worst Enemy"). Remember, once it's yours, you still need to perform the new position competently.

Allow me to share a modest success story about a woman I'll call Maria, a staff member at one of the stores where I functioned as manager. Maria started applying semi-annually to be in the training course for store management. If accepted, she would become a trainee and then in a few months be promoted to department manager. Candidates included both internal applicants and recent college graduates seeking a position. Maria was a very capable member of the sales staff, and had my recommendation as well of that of senior staff members. We felt she possessed all of the necessary qualifications to take the next step and be successful even though she didn't hold a university degree. The district HR manager and several other store managers interviewed the applicants. We continued recommending her for an interview every six months when the program cycle presented itself. She went through this screening process three times without being selected. On the third pass, the selection committee told us Maria would have made the program if they just had one more opening. It was very disappointing for her. We tried to build her up offering, "Your time will come. Keep trying. Don't quit." She handled it well and didn't complain, but I knew she was starting to wonder if it was worth the effort to go through all of the motions again, since it was both taxing and disheartening. After I transferred from the store to take another position, a member of the management team called to tell me that upon her fourth attempt, Maria was their top candidate and was offered a position.

Unless you're seeking something akin to an apprenticeship program, you're putting career steps in the wrong sequence if you hope to get a job and then later learn how to do it satisfactorily. Though we don't always see it this way, it's almost always better not to get the position you're pursuing if you're not ready to handle the demands. It's preferable to wait a while and become qualified for the opportunity so you can shine. What good is it if you get accepted, but then circumstances reveal you're not prepared to successfully handle certain job requirements? This could result in getting stuck in the position, demoted, or even fired. If you're not ready to handle major responsibilities, you're going to make major mistakes. When you do, upper management will take note and you'll have a dark cloud hanging over you. They'll wonder if you're going to succeed or if you need to be removed. Once you acquire a negative reputation, it takes considerable time to repair your image and regain senior management's confidence. In some instances, I've seen this take several years, if it happened at all.

When staff members working under my umbrella completed sub-standard work—especially when they repeated mistakes—I didn't forget it for some time. Not only did the job get done poorly, but it also reflected negatively on the rest of our team (see: "The Most Important Word"). This made me very hesitant to give them more chances if the event was still fresh in everyone's mind. If at some point later they're recommended by a staff member, their work performance is the first issue to discuss. Are they sure the failure won't be repeated and that we can trust them not to stumble in a major way again? I reassert that it's better for people to be placed in a job for which they're prepared or even over prepared so they can excel.

Being a little apprehensive or looking over our shoulder periodically is a good practice. Don't be caught off-guard being lazy or sloppy because you're overconfident. On the other hand, don't become so paranoid that you're a nervous wreck or annoying people making mountains out of molehills.

We've all seen cartoons where the main character has an angel on the right shoulder and a devil on the left, both replicas of themselves. In life, we sometimes get into a rut wherein a little voice whispers in our ear that we're a failure or that something bad is going to happen. By being conscious of this phenomenon, you can choose to shut off the negative feelings or undertones realizing that they're neither healthy nor in our best interest. There was a period in my career when several senior managers with whom I worked closely were terminated over a very short period. Every day for a couple of years thereafter, I went to work braced for the possibility that I might get let go. In retrospect, it was almost like being terminated hundreds of times. I would have been better off emotionally to have enjoyed the good things that life offers each day like accomplishing positive results regarding work, family, friends, and other pleasures, and just faced it once when and if it happened (it didn't). All of those coworkers who did lose their jobs continued on with their lives and many of them are happier for it. As King Arthur says in *Camelot*, "I'm too young and too old. Too old not to know that fears can be imaginary and too young not to be tormented by them."[16]

Part of being over prepared includes accumulating as much savings as you can without turning into Scrooge. Pay yourself and protect the fund you build. One of my high school teachers impressed upon me the importance of becoming independently wealthy: a term he defined as having enough money so you don't need to work for the rest of your life. If you haven't reached that financial state yet, another interim goal would be to have enough resources to weather a customary period of unemployment. This provides you peace of mind. It further allows you to be true to your values if you're asked to do something contrary to your moral compass.

As a final note, some individuals in sports, business, entertainment, or the like are recognized for individual achievements, but many others get good contracts because they fill an important niche for the group and know how to help make their team or business venture achieve success.

ALWAYS GIVE OUR BEST

This seems like counsel we shouldn't need, doesn't it? After all, we always contribute close to 100%, right? Sadly, I've witnessed talented professionals become demoralized, give up, or ramp back their efforts when they didn't get a promotion or recognition they felt they deserved. This was apparent in the way they slacked off their work responsibilities after they'd tendered their notice to accept another position. Previously they approached their assignment with vigor, but now they started working short days while leaving time-sensitive projects for their replacement. Someone coined the term "lame duck," which refers to a person who mentally checks out and becomes ineffective because their term is ending.

It's difficult for most associates to maintain a high level of respect for

---

[16] "*Camelot* (1967): Quotes." *IMDb*, 2023, imdb.com/title/tt0061439/quotes/?ref_=tt_trv_qu. Accessed 3 March 2023.

people who change their nature under these conditions. Remember that coworkers and senior management are observing and will usually resent it if tasks we should finish are left uncompleted, impacting the performance of the business. Even though we're leaving, we should still hope for associates to admire us (see: "The Power of Relationships" and "Seek Respect Before Friendship"). These last negative impressions may overshadow favorable feelings and inhibit others from notifying us of future job openings or wanting to work with us again (see: "Spend Goodwill, but Carefully"). It may even preclude them from giving us a great reference, or in some cases offering us a job, later on in our career.

The poet Maya Angelou advised her friend Oprah Winfrey, "That was when you [were] twenty. Now you're in your thirties. When you know better, you do better."[17] At the very least, we need to avoid bad habits that will keep us from succeeding at our next opportunity. Giving our best effort needs to be a routine practice. It's just what we do. If we allow ourselves excuses for holding back, we'll find that we don't give our best very often since there are so many justifications like thinking we're not being treated fairly, nobody is watching, or that we're rarely thanked for our efforts.

Shortcuts are another potential snare. Some are terrific time savers, but shun them unless they're authorized and a better way to get a quality job done in less time. Don't leave vital tasks undone (see: "Multi-Tasking: Virtue or Vice?"). Find a way to do the mundane, but important, undertakings even if they're not immediately urgent. This includes completing thoughtful reviews and budgets. Too many people don't perform these types of projects with the attention they deserve, sometimes justifying their actions by claiming that there has not been enough time allotted to conscientiously complete them.

---

[17] Quoted in "The Powerful Lesson Maya Angelou Taught Oprah." *OWN*, oprah.com/oprahs-lifeclass/the-powerful-lesson-maya-angelou-taught-oprah-video. Accessed 27 February 2023.

During my first year working for one of my employers, I was allotted two weeks to submit monetary plans for the 17 operational areas I felt needed financial delineation. Since this was my first effort creating them for these departments, at this company, and because they hadn't operated from budgets before (really!), it was apparent I couldn't just delegate this task to my management team. Working almost continually for that period and involving my leadership team to get their input, I turned in the budgets only to be informed that the company had decided to wait until the next year to implement detailed departmental budgets. Unusual as it was, they were concerned that once the monetary plans were published, each department would spend up to that amount while others exceeded their allotted resources. In other words, they were concerned about the lack of financial discipline among managerial staff.

This doesn't seem to make a good case for jumping on an assignment, but I held my tongue because I wasn't aware of all of the extenuating circumstances. That restraint and our efforts bought me goodwill with the controller (see: "The Most Important Word"). He knew I'd gone to great effort and he felt sheepish for having asked me to perform a challenging task that appeared to have been for naught. This also served me well in our future interactions. The next year the effort was almost a breeze because the groundwork had been laid and I'd already gone through the process.

To show you what I mean, when you have a handful of business plans to turn in (from as many functional disciplines), budgets from a dozen or so departments to formulate, reviews for seven or eight direct reports to write, and several hundred proposed raises to review, it may seem like it can't all be done in the time allotted. Keep in mind that there will usually be others who don't finish these tasks until after the deadline. However, that's not a good justification for you to perform these efforts poorly or past the due date. If you really need it, negotiate for more time in advance (see: "Overwhelming To-Do Lists").

As the old adage asserts, "There are no silver bullets." Most of us have also heard that "the devil is in the details" and "a job worth doing, is a job worth doing well" (which I first heard from my father). Mike Tyson, seemingly quoting American boxing coach Cus D'Amato who helped guide Floyd Patterson, José Torres, and Tyson to world titles, wrote, "Discipline is doing what you hate to do, but nonetheless doing it like you love it."[18] In good conscience, we need to carefully examine details contained in reports, wage recommendations, or the language found in contracts even though our superiors will probably never know until there's a glaring error. None of these types of duties should be a victim of neglect. When we don't give seemingly unimportant projects the attention they deserve, our team members, employer, and ourselves will all experience the unintended negative consequences (see: "Order Serves Success").

It's all of the little building blocks that build a foundation for success. Mother Teresa has been credited with saying, "If each of us would only sweep our own doorstep, the whole world would be clean."[19] We shouldn't ignore important small aspects just because there isn't a big push or mandate from upper management to do them. Napoleon Hill wrote, "If you cannot do great things yourself, remember that you may do small things in a great way."[20] Do the right things because you understand they ultimately have an important purpose (see: "Take the High Road"). Be the conscience and protector of morale. Champion continuous improvement. Ensure employee safety. These issues can't be left unaddressed because someone above didn't direct us to make them a priority or give us detailed

---

[18] @MikeTyson. "Discipline is doing what you hate to do, but nonetheless doing it like you love it. #miketyson." *Twitter*, 15 October 2018, 2:00 p.m., twitter.com/MikeTyson/status/1051925919710027777?lang=en.

[19] Teresa, Mother. "If each of us would only sweep our own doorstep, the whole world would be clean." *AZ Quotes*. 2023. azquotes.com/quote/811757. Accessed 3 March 2023.

[20] Hill, Napoleon. *The Law of Success: The Mast Wealth-Builder's Complete and Original Lesson Plan for Achieving Your Dreams*. Penguin Publishing Group, 2008. p. 50.

metrics to achieve. As one of my supervisors once shared, "Part of her job is to figure out what her job is."

INFLUENCING IMPRESSIONS

An item worthy of discussion is analyzing the attitudes we portray. Let's face it, cheerleaders have definite intrinsic value, not just to spectators or most sports teams wouldn't have them. More often than we realize, we can personally assume that role if we try. This isn't to suggest that we should attempt to be someone we're not, but in our own way we can be as enthusiastic, optimistic, and encouraging as possible. If you're charismatic, thank your lucky stars and any life coaches who have helped you develop this attribute. If you're not naturally charming, then you're like me, but hopefully you don't share some of my less desirable attributes including my low, monotone voice.

For one, if we can't accept an assignment enthusiastically, then we should at least do so agreeably. Ownership and upper management wants employees who are "all in." They want team players who will give everything possible to take the enterprise forward. Be excited about the possibilities and committed to the journey. Furthermore, no one should try to create a good impression by disparaging others. It rarely works. Those who know me can attest that I need to improve in this area.

Do your best to display confidence, something else with which I struggled early in life. Working as a sales manager in a home store (with merchandise like furniture and appliances), the man who hired me and who was the director over that division called me and asked me what were we doing giving away free televisions? This was obviously a false claim and he certainly knew it. Totally caught by surprise, my first response was something like, "I'm not aware of any sales people doing that." This was followed by absolute silence on his end. I took the bait, so I next offered in a higher voice, "Where is this complaint coming from? There must be some misunderstanding." Once again there was a very pregnant pause, with no response.

If I was breathing, it certainly wasn't deeply. My vocal cords tightened with stress, and I had a healthy dose of fear for my job. I felt like I was standing on a precipice; as each moment ticked by, I was moving closer to the cliff's edge. My final response came out both shrill and weak as I promised to investigate immediately and call him back. He must have enjoyed every moment of this. It was then and there that I promised myself to never fall into the trap of humiliating myself when caught off guard again, especially when being baited. I wasn't guiding his impressions of me in the way that I hoped. Interestingly, I must have improved because he later became the president of another firm and hired me once more (maybe for entertainment purposes).

Problems aren't something I enjoy. The reason I take them on and try to fix them is because they honestly annoy me, and I want to make them go away—permanently. Life has taught me that when I can get others to join in this endeavor, the probability of success is much, much greater. I've also grown to understand that my chance of enlisting others increases if I show enthusiasm, a positive attitude, and incorporate grace under pressure. This is another trait that requires my attention. Although I'm eager to overcome obstacles, I get frustrated that others created this condition that could have been avoided. When life or work is exasperating, project optimism and assurance that everything will work out. We also need to swiftly get over whatever emotions we feel towards what caused the situation. Who wants to follow a pessimist—or in my case, a complainer—into battle? If only I could remember to apply that concept daily. Join me as I continue my lifelong quest to work harder at looking on the bright side, welcoming challenges instead of becoming defensive, and smiling as much as possible (see: "Smile and be Approachable"). Let's be vigilant about not spreading negativity, since it sucks the life (or at least the joy and motivation) out of those who surround us. Rather, we should portray confidence, enthusiasm, and the energy to tackle the challenges our teams face.

Another aspect of influencing impressions involves appearance. As it relates to our personal look, we should be dressed in suitable clothing to do our job and present ourselves in an orderly and well-groomed manner (there are some obvious exceptions like rockstars, I suppose) even if our job requires us to get dirty.

Additionally, understand that how our operational space looks—especially the areas first encountered—has a lot of impact on how a significant percentage of our visitors perceive us and our portion of the organization. This ranges from building grounds to lobbies and offices. When I enter a distribution center, the first thing I look at is how the business takes care of their merchandise and equipment. Is product lying on the floors broken or damaged? If standards are low, complaints and allegations will mushroom at the first poor inventory or service failure. The evidence was in plain sight (see: "Set Higher Standards" and "The Most Important Word"). Thankfully, our operational units received a lot of mileage over the years when guests came into our facilities and saw that they were neat and organized. We referred to it as always being "visit ready." If guests are from departments like accounting or purchasing, they're not immediately concerned about how much merchandise or product we were damaging or losing.

This applies to any place of business. Some people may not notice if there are weeds and trash in the parking lot or if the furniture and carpet in the waiting area are stained or dirty, but there's a considerable portion of the population who will. Having worked with peers whose offices were in a state of disarray, adorned by unkempt stacks of reports, outdated objects, and even trash, was I surprised when they didn't remember an assignment or hit a deadline (see: "Order Serves Success")? Many people will combine performance indicators with their visual observations of an unkempt space and label a department or team member as disorganized or ineffectual.

When I went to interview with one large firm, I probably should have seen what I was getting into and run away. My office would be in the primary distribution facility, several hundred square feet in size. The structure looked much older than it was. During a tour of the facility, I saw a few racking shelves that had failed under too much weight and there was dust, trash, and damaged product collecting underneath. The floors were stained in areas and hadn't been resealed for years. The unmistakable vibe was that the staff didn't have any interest in housekeeping or protecting the merchandise. It was quite unimpressive.

When team members have visited a third-party warehouse operation under consideration for use in a new or developing market, initial impressions were a huge factor in our decision about whether we wanted to contract their services. We weren't going to trust them with our company's merchandise if they weren't protecting their other clients' property. We inferred they would also have a higher than acceptable error rate in shipping out orders and would be using up or exceeding any product shortage dollar allowance for damage and loss that would be built into the agreement. If they treated merchandise with such indifference, why would we believe any promises about their stellar performance record?

One day, an accounting department executive performed an inspection of our Arizona distribution center. They hadn't visited our facility for at least a year, and it was their first thorough walkthrough since I'd been employed. When the walkthrough was finished, they stated, "I saw tens of thousands of dollars' worth of damaged merchandise." Afterwards, upon arriving back at headquarters, they reported these concerns to my boss and the owner.

This facility held about $18 million dollars of merchandise in 350,000 square feet (keep in mind that the product was inexpensive and often bulky). Orders were filled by staff members driving around the warehouse on "order pickers" (specialized lifts), and manually transferring cases of merchandise from the racking onto a pallet sitting on the forks of this equipment. An employee needed to drive the lift they were operating close to the rack, and then elevate the order picker to various height levels where the cross beams were holding individual pallets of identical products. Sometimes a carton, sticking out too far on one of the lower levels, would get rubbed by the equipment, damaging a few items inside the case.

As soon as the accounting executive left, an asset protection staff member was located and instructed to walk throughout the facility and make a list of all of the non-saleable merchandise he could find. His inspection totaled approximately $1,200 worth of product that had been damaged since the last inventory six months previously. Be aware that he didn't do the assignment exactly as requested, since he estimated the damage rather than performing a detailed count (see: "Was it the Assignment Given?"). Once I had the estimate in hand, I shared it with my boss, the owner, and the accounting executive who responded, "No, that's not correct." Immediately upon returning to the distribution center, the asset protection team member was directed to go back again, with another employee, and make an actual list as I'd originally requested. We needed to put this matter to rest as soon as possible. The revised amount was less than three thousand dollars. Although this was concerning, it certainly didn't approach "tens of thousands of dollars." *Note: The average shortage for the four annual inventories that followed was only two-tenths of one percent.*

The moral of the story is that if we had handled these minor damages daily, the issue would never have been blown out of proportion. We implemented the system we should have had all along, pulling damaged items to a central and secure location. Then we had asset protection record the unsalvageable items on a log before disposing of them on a timely basis. Finally, all entries were tracked for management to compare to last year's losses. *Note: The best course of action is to perform a Six Sigma-like project, investigating the origin of the problem and then mandating retraining or creating a new procedure to eliminate as much of the damage as possible. Don't allow this type of damaged product to accumulate anywhere, including a trash can or dumpster where staff members can see it and may be tempted to help themselves (for reasons I won't elaborate).*

Always be mindful of the verbal and non-verbal signals we send to those around us. The obstacles and undertakings we face will be demanding enough, in and of themselves, without adding undesirable perceptions to the equation.

WAS IT THE ASSIGNMENT GIVEN?

Allow me to acknowledge how frustrating it is to give a directive and then find out down the road that the duty was abandoned because it was tiresome or inconvenient. This includes instances when direct reports no longer monitor accuracy, fail to ensure safety practices are followed, or don't coach employees who are performing outside of established standards. When you encounter this condition, it places more value on putting standard operating practices into place and then requiring status reports as an element of your follow-up (see: "Identify and Monitor Pulse Points").

As you undoubtedly understand, because of life experiences and individual frame of reference, words don't mean the same to everyone. Thus, the individuals you're communicating with frequently don't always comprehend some of the concepts or information you're sharing even if they captured a portion of the spirit that was intended. Solicit and listen to coworkers' feedback and then restate the assignment until everyone involved aligns on the details of the issue at hand. Be assured, I've wasted others' time and my own by not following this more thoroughly and taking a little longer to communicate. Have you heard the adage, "Go slow so you can go fast"? You don't want to waste time executing a task incorrectly. The results can vary, either from being totally off target to close to the original objective but still needing another pass to tidy up. It doesn't hurt for a team to agree that over-communicating is preferable to under-communicating. This adds a healthy dose of foresight to the equation. If you want to ensure the outcome winds up even better, confer early in the process. An illustration: When conducting an inventory, it's crucial to check the first inventory sheet from every counting pair in detail. It's not good for an inventory team to count for hours and then, when their work is checked by a manager assigned to auditing, send the duo back to redo all their work to that point.

Performing the complete assignment given impacts trustworthiness as well (see: "The Most Important Word"). This means the responsibility for clarification rests with both parties. If you don't comprehend precisely what the delegator wants, ask. If you still don't get a clear answer, observe, listen, and collect clues and evidence to align yourself with their intentions. When you walk in the boss' office to deliver a report, they're going to be let down to find out what you're giving them is either incomplete, or even worse, totally off the mark. Even if they fail to check up on you, for projects of any length you should clarify objectives in order to understand the original mission. Then, take initiative to be in contact early on to confirm you're headed in the right direction. Sometimes the need that originated an assignment will change in a matter of hours. If your supervisor's efforts to update or redirect you were delayed or overlooked, you're the one who will be doing extra, unnecessary work.

In a related vein, we should report in an appropriate manner to our boss (email, weekly status meetings, texts, sticky notes, etc.) when a task has been completed or we've become aware of a problem of which they should be informed. Visualize your boss walking down the executive wing of your headquarters encountering another executive who says something like, "Why isn't the new lease space ready for my department to move into yet?" or "Did you know that the warehouse didn't assemble any new customer introductory kits yesterday and we're out of stock?" If your supervisor can't answer because you haven't armed them with the facts, it makes them look like they're out of touch (see: "The Most Important

Word" and "Respond Quickly"), or more dramatically, that they showed up to a gunfight without ammunition.

Another complication can arise if we haven't differentiated between what elements of the job we enjoy working on as opposed to focusing on what it is that our boss wants us to accomplish. Perhaps you're an engineer who enjoys design work or a marketing specialist that likes branding. Be careful not to be so immersed in that one area that you don't spend enough time with your other job responsibilities, like monitoring the performance of your team, meeting individually with direct reports, or financial planning.

This also pertains to when we receive requests to supply data or information. Answer the question that was asked and add any additional pertinent facts or material. It's very frustrating for a director to send out a communiqué, ask for specific data, and then sort through a rambling, unorganized response only to realize that they must send an email or a phone message to get the original questions answered. This can be avoided if the details initially requested are available in our first response.

CLARIFY WITHOUT DISPLAYING IGNORANCE

Asking questions is a great time saver: we can gain knowledge, avoid unnecessary fact checking or research, and make sure we carry out the assignment in the right way the first time. However, there's also an art to asking questions that has eluded me at times. My temperament leads me to say things like, "I don't have a clue how an internal combustion engine works," even though I understand some of the basics. Instead, I should ask, "Would you be kind enough to rehearse the finer details of the stroke sequence for this engine?" By doing so, we're not pretending to know something we don't, but we're also allowing for what knowledge we do have. It's also a courtesy to the respondent since they can frame their answer to better match our understanding.

Even if we can't ask the question correctly, in most situations it's still better to inquire. Just make sure to listen and take careful notes, if necessary, to remember what we're being told, so we don't have to repeat the same inquiry yet again. One of the most frequent complaints I hear about new hires is how many times they have to be retrained on the same subject matter.

As a final thought, we should spend some effort "managing our manager." Accomplish this by studying and understanding their style and approach to responsibilities. Then we'll know in what format they like proposals presented to them, what time of day they prefer to meet, or when they're most amenable to fielding questions. This facilitates getting the answers or resources we need from them. Don't confuse this with manipulation—we're not withholding or distorting information (see: "Planting Seeds"). Instead, we're in tune and honoring their preferences.

SEEK AND APPLY ADVICE

Most people are only too happy to offer their advice, often when nobody asks. On the other hand, very few people are willing to ask for feedback and then listen. Why do people insist on learning things the hard way? Why will a grown child go out and purchase a piece of property on their own when they have someone close to them who is an architect, construction foreman, or appraiser who could offer concrete guidance regarding the value and conditions of buying?

Large or small, there's usually some disparity between our perception of how we perform and our boss's perception of how we perform. Our supervisor's impressions are what they are, regardless if we understand them or not. Just as in fighting a serious medical diagnosis, our best chance of success comes from gathering the facts and then intelligently dealing with them. Not wanting to know how we're doing or what is expected of us isn't a valid reason to not ask. We can't fix the problem, or explain why we're not hitting the mark, without first identifying the origin of the gap.

Be bold and wise enough to ask if there's any room for improvement in your job performance. Suppose you solicit input and your boss replies you should be at work every morning by 8:00 a.m. Begin by coming to grips with the reality that they'll always be irritated about your schedule. Next, your options are to: (a) ignore the feedback and accept that it will remain an issue; (b) choose to correct the objectionable behavior; or (c) ask for an explanation of their reasoning and discuss if there are other ways to address the concern. Using this last approach, the resolution may be an agreement that you will only take a 30-minute lunch or stay a half hour later than everyone else.

We can't learn anything if we believe we already know everything. Likewise, we'll never improve if we can't accept coaching. There have been dozens of times when I've offered a suggestion to staff members about how to handle a worrisome circumstance, and I just knew as they were leaving my office they weren't going to try it (see: "Find a Mentor"). They'd already determined it wasn't going to work. A closed-minded attitude is a huge detriment to personal growth.

One trainee with whom I worked was an exception to the rule. She would come into my office and we would have a good discussion about how to tackle a situation. Of course, I would make recommendations about how to handle the issue since I love to give advice (you figured that out quite a few pages ago). At first, I was surprised when she returned and said, "It didn't work quite the way you said it would, but I adapted it to the situation, and I think things are going to be okay." She was willing to look at the essence of the suggestion and figure out how to apply it to the circumstance at hand. She would then evaluate the solution's effectiveness while deciding how to fine-tune the approach the next time she faced a similar problem. When she reported back to me, I also learned from her adaptation and navigation. We both benefitted.

There was another very fine person with whom I worked. He was older than me by about 15 years and preferred not to make any changes until he had seen, as he put it, "the whole cycle" (an entire year). My impression was that if I couldn't get him to make changes with areas that weren't running smoothly, one or both of us would lose our job. We didn't have the luxury of waiting that long to turn things around. It's a bit like coaching in professional sports: many new coaches are given three- or four-year contracts. If they have a losing season or two without making notable gains, they're fired. The owner wants to see progress and they want to see it soon.

If something doesn't work, scrap it after you've given it a reasonable amount of effort and time: "That didn't work, let's try something else." It's a reasonable guarantee that a manager who tries new approaches will have enough successes amid limited failures to achieve a net positive result. A manager who won't accept advice from the boss or try well thought-out changes from their team will never see any significant development or progress. Work hard, but also work as intelligently as possible.

It's an important practice to seek feedback from staff. At several different employers, leadership teams of which I was a part held roundtables with different departments. Refreshments were served, and we kicked things off by sharing upcoming plans or recent improvements to prime the participation pump. If no one offered feedback, we would ask questions to solicit opinions on matters we knew were current issues with staff. Abbreviated notes were taken and posted for everyone in the facility to read so they could see that management was committed to carrying out programs to improve working conditions. Even better, when a difficulty that staff had called out was fixed promptly, we could publicize the success when the next recap was posted. There were periods where we engaged in this practice for years, but I confess we never held these roundtables as often as we should have.

When seeking peer or subordinate feedback, keep in mind that a coworker's real feelings are not often expressed candidly when confronted in person. On separate occasions, a couple of professionals didn't get the promotions they thought were theirs. Their next move was to go around and ask coworkers if they enjoyed working together and if they felt they were competent. The outcome was predictable. Peers halfheartedly expressed their backing without sharing any of the frustrations or criticism I'd fielded earlier. *Note: Many people won't tell you the truth when they're confronted face-to-face and sense you already have an answer or are unwilling to accept their opinions.*

Avail yourself of 360-degree evaluation programs since they're very informative and somewhat more confidential. These assessments include direct feedback from an employee's subordinates, supervisor, and colleagues. It can also include feedback from customers and suppliers.

Over time, make it a point to identify who gives you the best advice (see: "Find a Mentor"). One man with whom I worked spent an inordinate amount of time asking others' opinions. It took me a while to understand that when he got advice he didn't like, he'd keep searching until he found someone to appease and validate his views no matter how much the topic was outside of their area of expertise. My guidance to him was to identify a few capable managers whom he could trust based on the success of applying their advice, and then focus on their counsel.

PAYING YOUR DUES

Coworkers aware of the circumstances surrounding our hiring expect us to be qualified to perform our role. One executive I knew moved from graduate school into a trainee position with an established retail chain. These trainee assignments typically lasted from three to nine months unless there were major performance concerns. The individual became impatient, I suppose, and left the firm before getting assigned a non-trainee role. Their next position was with their family-owned business, in the northwest, as a senior manager. There was some resentment on the part of the supervisory staff because it seemed this new VP hadn't gained enough experience or knowledge of the discipline in order to jump in and lead. If you find yourself in this position, the best thing you can do is carry your share of the load, involve others in decisions when their expertise or position justifies it, and be appreciative of others who are helping the team succeed. You might also consider a strategy to expand your title and responsibilities as you gain experience. Over time, this will steadily amplify your authenticity (see: "The Most Important Word").

A man I once worked with told me a joke that relates to this: the owner of a firm called in a new worker, praised him for turning around the mailroom in just a few weeks, then gave him a big promotion. The owner later profusely complimented his prodigy for orchestrating a successful overhaul of the entire sales division in just a few months, to which the employee responded, "Gee, thanks, Dad."

Most of us work so hard to complete our education or training that we think life will get much better when all of the homework, tests, and financial hardship are in the rearview mirror. At least that's how I, "Mr. Naïve," thought it would be. I was going to start making lots of money instead of paying most of my meager income to the university. What I didn't realize was how much living off-campus was going to cost in relationship to my take-home pay. Housing, transportation, insurance, and utilities all got more expensive, especially since my wife and I had a small family to feed and support. We'd just exchanged the obstacles associated with the formal education phase of life for a different set of challenges associated with making a living and establishing ourselves financially.

After our children finished college, a piece of advice I didn't give them was what to expect in their first job. That reality would come soon enough. It just wasn't in my heart to tell my kids that life was still going to be hard, only in a different way. I saved my insight until in due course they shared their concerns about their new professions. My method was the same as a surgeon who doesn't tell you too much about the difficulty of post-surgery recovery, in case you decide you don't want to go through with the procedure. The physician is hopeful the surgery will ultimately make your life better and doesn't want to scare you off.

The following story demonstrates how to willingly perform in order to justify compensation when presented with a new employment opportunity (see: "Earn More Than We're Paid"). We once made an offer to a young part-time employee who had just finished an engineering degree. We offered him the title of assistant engineer and mapped out a path to full engineer, along with respectable, frequent pay increases. He considered the offer an affront and rejected it despite receiving assurance from several managers and human resources that this short-term career path would be honored if he progressed as expected. We offered the same deal to a young woman with a similar resume who jumped at the chance. The first person left the company but then came back in a similar role to the one he'd occupied previously, but not as the assistant engineer. The other individual became a full engineer in a couple of years and was way ahead of the first in both compensation and career path. The original candidate moved up within his department, but never into the engineer role that he wanted. I lost track when he subsequently left again, hopefully to a position better matched to his expectations.

Paying your dues is generally a combination of three unspoken strategies on the part of the employer. First, they want to see how willing you are to do whatever it takes to help the enterprise be successful. Second, giving you less-desirable duties is an initiation, sparing the hiring supervisor and more senior staff from tasks they performed previously. Third, there's knowledge to be gained from carrying out these mundane or time-consuming assignments, making you more effective. Your firm knows that in time you'll expect to be excluded from some of these unpleasant projects as they pass to the new freshman class, so to speak. Realize that some of the frustrations you're exposed to during the first few years of your career will subside noticeably over time. As one example, you usually won't be asked to move around and work undesirable schedules as often.

BIG FISH, LITTLE POND

Graduating college and eager to land a position in a Fortune 500 firm, I figured the larger the company the greater the opportunity and compensation. My first job after grad school was with a large retail company, but after that my course seemed to drift in a counter-intuitive direction for the next segment of my career. After working for that department store, my next move was to a women's high-fashion house carrying designer labels like Gucci. From there, the next stop was a specialty discounter, then back to a department store, before moving to a start-up dollar store venture. Toward the end of this journey in retail, I joked with my wife that my next stop might be cranking an organ grinder—monkey included—on the street corner.

After working in the business world for many years, when I checked in with a program director he asked if I could afford this kind of occupational "markdown" (as he saw my employment pattern to that point). I felt like he was saying that I was unwisely moving away from more prestigious retail firms.

Although a lot of my training was fine-tuned with the "big boys" in retail working in specialty positions, I soon realized the valuable learning and exposure I gained in the two smaller ventures I worked at in college. Later on, the reality was that I did better financially in a key role with entrepreneurial companies than I did languishing as a middle manager in older, established firms. Even more telling was that some of these fledgling enterprises ended up flourishing into substantial businesses. Opening a warehouse as part of a select task force at a large corporation was nowhere near as satisfying as opening a distribution center when I was the most senior supply chain/operations manager in a non-Fortune 500 company. Within the developing firm, our small yet capable group could mold the fresh clay in our hands as we developed and built our sensible state-of-the-art facilities, rivaling bigger logistics centers in performance and innovation.

To summarize, a small company equals less bureaucracy, more influence, and greater flexibility while providing broader responsibilities you might not experience as rapidly in a huge operation. Also, stock ownership or options in a start-up can be worth more than in an established company. This isn't to suggest an employment prospect in a large company is ill-advised. Rather, I'm offering that a position in a smaller operation can provide rewarding opportunities if the concept, leadership team, and financial backing are impressive. Weigh all of the factors—including pension plans offered by larger firms—and as you would do in playing a game of pool, always consider your next move.

FIND A MENTOR

When I was working as a store manager, the vice president of operations sent word through HR that he wanted a few managers from the store division to accept positions in the distribution centers. He felt this cross-pollination would help logistics better understand and serve its customers, the stores. It was a thoughtful initiative. The next clear promotional opportunity in my career path was to become an assistant general merchandise manager, regularly visiting all of the stores to oversee the merchandising of categories like domestics, cosmetics, and men's clothing. Time working as a buyer had convinced me that I didn't want to travel that much in a job again, so this alternative path appealed to me. Having already worked in and enjoyed operations, it was exciting to secure a position as a divisional manager in the new distribution center. The facility was to be built about 40 miles from my current store.

Everything seemed to be going well as I participated in the project from the ground up. I got along well with the VP (my boss's boss) and felt he might be a possible mentor who would take personal interest in my development. Suddenly, we were stunned to learn this senior manager had left the company and would be replaced by someone we didn't know. Now, I would be only one of a dozen divisional managers operating in three distribution centers companywide. Had I made the right move, or was I doomed to get lost in the shuffle?

Later, the new VP told me I needed to gain experience outside of the company to prepare myself to be considered for a promotion to director. This was around the same time we were encouraged to look at ways to improve the operation. When I presented this new administrator with a couple different analyses I'd taken on without being assigned, she looked at the title of the document and said, "I already have someone working on that," and handed it back to me. Some years after I left to accept a director's position elsewhere, I applied for a director position with this previous employer; it was an attempt to get our growing family back closer to their grandparents. That same VP reversed her earlier advice and told me that she wanted to fill the position from within, since the need called for someone currently immersed in my former company's systems and culture. Clearly, each time an attempt was being made to tactfully inform yours truly that there wasn't interest in placing me as a key member of the leadership team. Working as a divisional manager at that company drastically changed as I went from having a helpful contact and supporter to working for someone who had no interest in my career.

Having a mentor can range from periodic coaching to teacher-and-student association. I've had several of the former, but only one of the latter. That single relationship provided me with more concrete tools to succeed than several others combined. Looking back, I sincerely wish I'd tried harder to turn more of these other affiliations into a more robust mentorship (see: "Seek and Apply Advice").

Typically, the person you report to is in the best position to see what's keeping you from getting ahead. It's much easier to advance when you have a boss that appreciates your loyalty, your endeavors, and is willing to invest in your development. Go out of your way to ask for your supervisor's feedback, not only on your current performance but on how to achieve your full potential as well. Ask how you can help them by performing your job better. Listen and be appreciative of direction, especially when it's candid (the best type). Then, demonstrate you're truly trying to improve your contribution by applying their advice.

Since mentoring involves considerable effort and energy, many people are simply unwilling to pursue or embrace these relationships. The best managers make the best candidates when you're seeking guidance. You need somebody who can show you the ropes and look out for you. This is a two-way street. People don't generally adopt other people and put them under their wing entirely out of the goodness of their heart—it's symbiotic. They gravitate to people who are doing a good job and who will help them accomplish meaningful goals. Top-notch managers want to be surrounded by employees that come through in a bind and get the job done. Sure, they may enjoy if you're funny or charming, but don't expect to be picked first in the real game of business if that's the best you can offer.

In a business setting, tutors need students who are teachable and willing to be corrected so they don't waste their time. It's part of a chain. If the mentor is going to move up, they need somebody who helps them look good and who can effectively replace them. They want to develop staff who has their back and can assist them in achieving success at the next level. Likewise, workers need to coach and grow junior supervisory staff so considerable success can be accomplished throughout the department.

Having a healthy connection with an advisor requires humility; trying to come across as all-knowing to superiors often gets in the way. Perhaps if I'd sought out my supervisors' counsel more frequently, they would have seen opportunities to tutor me on other occasions without an invitation. Likewise, I've experienced circumstances when I was trying to counsel and help someone avoid a pitfall and I've been ignored and snubbed. It certainly discouraged me from trying to coach that same individual in the future.

More than once, I've encountered a member of the organization who was clearly more intelligent than their peers, at least as it pertained to having technical knowledge in a specialty area. Even though they were smart, these staff members shared a few undesirable characteristics that made it difficult to form a synergetic link. They would: (a) act unilaterally when others needed to be either involved or informed regarding such matters as work instructions given to vendors; (b) exhibit poor follow-up on small or medium assignments, often requiring second or third reminders; and (c) come in late and leave work early without informing anyone of their whereabouts. *Note: Sure, they worked long hours on occasion, but so did most of their peers.* At some point, these employees likely grew weary of hearing the same issues in reviews or private conversations. Universally, they wanted to be promoted. At appropriate opportunities, I attempted to express my belief that these performance issues would be an obstacle for them regardless of the firm. Usually, these talented, yet un-coachable professionals left after a few years and were relatively successful in other endeavors better matched to their skills and aspirations. If you don't want to change, understand the possible consequences while also evaluating your career options. After all, it's your life.

WHAT POTENTIAL EMPLOYERS SEEK

Every interviewer or potential employer has their own set of criteria for the applicants with whom they interact. The list of basic characteristics I'm seeking has changed very little over the years and I hope it's representative of what you may encounter. Certainly, the following qualities are desired by most reputable employers. A prospective candidate should be:

- A good communicator; tactful, while able to call out unaddressed concerns.
- Teachable and unpretentious; willing to receive constructive criticism.

- Conscientious; someone who won't leave assignments unfinished.
- Analytical and able to see opportunities and challenges on their own.
- Full of common sense.
- Sensitive of the need to get along well with others, so refereeing isn't required.
- Very productive and high energy; passionate about their work and able to ignite that passion within coworkers, clients, etc. *Note: Trainers need to not only be nurturing, communicative, and accurate, but they also need to demonstrate the upper reaches of the possible pace. If they're too methodical, it will create a setting where timeliness and productivity suffer.*
- Dedicated and loyal.
- Technically very capable, if that's required in their prospective role.

I encourage you to consider the validity of the items on this list and contemplate how you measure up.

INTERVIEW WHEN INVITED

Always be aware of attractive career options, even if you're content with your present situation. Thoughtfully consider interviewing with other organizations when given the opportunity. The exception would be if you're doing it so frequently it calls attention to itself. This keeps you prepared for the time when finding a different job is imperative. Besides, in the process of your visit you may learn something that will benefit your current firm.

If after the first meeting you determine you're not interested in the opportunity, be careful how far you go down the path with follow-up interviews. For one thing, it comes across as disingenuous to the prospective employer and could leave a bad impression should you encounter them in business dealings down the road. Accepting a first appointment says you're intrigued with what they may have to offer. Consenting to subsequent interviews indicates you're genuinely intent in trying to facilitate a match. If you withdraw your name after several meetings, the company courting you may feel you unfairly wasted their valuable time.

If you're exploring other prospects just to get an offer to submit to your current organization, be advised that asking them to counter should be done rarely, perhaps only once. If you accept your existing employer's counteroffer, remember you've used up some of your accumulated goodwill (see: "Spend Goodwill, but Carefully"). Consequently asking for or using up favors will create magnified resentment and you don't want that reputation. If later on you get a second job offer from another business, don't be surprised if your present firm chooses not to negotiate (see: "When and How to Negotiate").

By the way, one of the best questions you can offer when interviewing is, "What can I do to help your organization be even more successful?" This suggests that you get the big picture and that you're focused on contributing to—and not just landing—a job (see: "Earn More Than We're Paid").

SECTION TWO

LEADERSHIP & MANAGEMENT

WOULD YOU FOLLOW SOMEONE LIKE YOURSELF?

How would you like to work for a person with your personality and skill set? If you have doubts, it indicates you have some degree of sensitivity to your weaknesses which is much better than thinking you're above reproach. Try to move ahead quickly by focusing on how you can improve. Why shouldn't you be a catalyst that can make good things transpire at work, at home, or in the community? Why shouldn't you come to appreciate that you can brighten a room by projecting humble confidence? If this persona is backed by concern for others and a commitment to being practical and fair, you can achieve a great deal of good (see: "Smile and be Approachable").

For our style to be effective, it's important that it's consistent and understandable. Strive to be predictable so people can foresee what we hope to accomplish and incorporate the guidelines vital to these endeavors. Staff must have input into what is monitored so nothing important goes overlooked. Always ask them for the same kinds of information (new requests can be added), so they know what's important to us and what should be important to them. This includes everything from metrics in monthly reports, to inquiries about business plan progress, to safety or morale.

If people figure out what we need to know, they'll be better prepared to pursue the proper undertakings, accomplish them, and subsequently share that information. Good employees adjust their performance to match honorable expectations (see: "Three Types of Workers"). They not only want to answer pertinent questions, they want to perform well and report positive results. We need to be sure we don't have any blind spots. If we've identified the right pulse points, regularly make relevant inquiries, and require comprehensive reporting, we train members of the department to achieve commendable results (see: "Identify and Monitor Pulse Points").

A leader and their team can't achieve significant performance if they haven't envisioned the end target. Sights should be set high (see: "Set Higher Standards"). A primary role is to make certain the unit formulates plans based on corporate goals and objectives, and then successfully carries out these tactics and strategies. In some circumstances, the boss (meaning, us) must assess and then share what more should and shouldn't be done based on this mission statement.

There once was an occasion when an employee approached me at a store I was managing and requested that I personally authorize some expensive improvements he felt we needed. They'd been listening to some lecture series on leadership and challenged me to be more of a leader and make them happen. They were undoubtedly disappointed when I said my title was store manager and not store leader. My interpretation of the role was that my employer wanted me to manage staffing, merchandise presentation, ad set-up, inventory, and other defined duties. In this role, it wasn't my job to propose broad new initiatives. Nevertheless, I should have seen myself as more of a leader within the boundaries of my environment, even if it was just to empower my team to find better methods to achieve the mission we'd been given. We did achieve noteworthy success, but we could have accomplished even more (see: "Set Higher Standards").

A coach should want to win every game. There should never be games they're willing to lose. However, they should remain positive, optimistic, and supportive when wins don't happen. Seek an understanding of which activities help facilitate success. Experience helps us learn these lessons. Then, once we genuinely believe in those disciplines and approaches, tactfully and persuasively share them with everyone involved, at a suitable time, so they can be brought into play. Keep work strategy obtainable but high, even though sometimes the team will fall short. Remember that any organized group will rarely exceed their goals, so you shouldn't lower the bar to meet sub-standard performance (see: "Set Higher Standards"). As a team member, what would it mean if the coach said, "Well, we've lost two of our first four games, so let's scrap our goal to win the division championship and just try to win half of the games we have left"? Objectives like striving to be world-class, having no lost-time accidents, and avoiding any incident of sexual harassment should not be negotiable goals.

A leader needs to be optimistic and project conviction and assurance. The team may be limited by our personal inadequacies, so be aware and try to compensate for them. Otherwise, personnel may only be as fast, as exacting, or as passionate as we model. This explains why the lead horse or sled dog is so critical to the success of the entire unit.

Desired results almost always follow correct behaviors. Be fair and supportive. Be the person who gets the most out of everyone; don't be the lone wolf. Make sure the department has the necessary resources while guiding execution without stifling ingenuity. When execution is complete, the work group should come together and evaluate what went well and what didn't. Soon thereafter, get everyone engaged in the next wave or cycle. Plan. Execute. Evaluate. And, oh yes, celebrate (appropriately and respectably).

Permit me to offer one final insight. We must all come to grips with the reality that we're not what people think of us. We're not whom people see us with. We're not what we own or possess. We're not what we do to make a living. We're not the title on our business card. In the eyes of our Creator, we're the good and noble that we embrace and help accomplish.

HANDLING A CRISIS

The first step to avoiding a crisis is to have a contingency plan. Consider crises types and group them according to the resources required to respond. Next, document and tailor available assets at your disposal like staff, equipment, open floor space, temporary utility sources, alternative processing techniques, personnel protection measures/gear, communication methods, and so on according to logical calamity category. If appropriate, this should include third-party providers committed to providing necessary services or materials on short notice to keep you operational. When you've created this document, even though things won't work out exactly as predicted, facing large obstacles tends to turn out much better if you have a safety net in place.

When confronted with a real or apparent disaster, try to assess and understand the obstacle quickly. Gather your supervisory team rapidly and allow your experts to provide insight and perform something akin to a medical triage. Then try and stop or at least control the bleeding. If a piece of machinery is putting out excessive defects, don't allow it to continue running. If facts are clear, address them immediately.

Don't confuse what you think with what you know. If a cause is unclear, don't put elaborate solutions in motion without confirming the facts. Guessing at causes and then implementing solutions based on false assumptions can be a huge waste of resources, including squandered time. It has never been said better than by Ed Harris' character in *Apollo 13*: "Let's work the problem, people. Let's not make things worse by guessing."[21] The exception is if preventative measures are obvious; if so, apply as many as

---

[21] "*Apollo 13* (1995): Quotes." *IMDb*, 2023, imdb.com/title/tt0112384/quotes/?ref_=tt_trv_qu. Accessed 3 March 2023.

you can swiftly. Case in point: if you have a house fire and can shut off the natural gas, do so immediately. Even if it's not currently providing fuel to the blaze, it could become part of the equation with disastrous consequences.

Thereafter, clearly communicate if this crisis takes precedent over other efforts. Assign specific individuals to distinct tasks (include these details in your contingency plan when practical). Make it clear how often and by what means your team should report back. It's extremely beneficial to establish short and well-timed update meetings or conference calls to keep key staff members informed and reallocate resources. Task supervisors with regularly updating their staff as the situation dictates. Remember, at this point in time your goal is to fix the problem and not the blame (see: "The Blame Game").

One possible approach is to blitz the difficulty, dividing the major damage control initiatives so you can conquer the problem. This last technique was permanently impressed upon my mind just after accepting a position with a firm out west. One of the processing areas known as "hardlines" (less-personal items such as appliances, electronics, or sporting goods often shipped in boxes) got slammed and it was taking three weeks to process orders. The processing manager was very dedicated to their job, but quite reactive and ineffective in a crisis. With over 15 years of service to the company, disqualification of this individual, at that firm, would take longer than I might be there myself. When faced with this predicament, I worried I might be terminated any day and I'd just relocated my family back across the country. One of the other managers in our team—a resourceful character—had run the area previously and asked if I would like advice. "I would love any suggestions," I told him. He said when this used to happen to him, the staff was split into three groups of similar size. Group #1 was asked to work on orders that were hot rushes, like merchandise for upcoming ads. Group #2 was assigned to work on orders that were bulky and taking up a lot of valuable warehouse floor space. Group #3 was assigned to orders based on date of first-in-first-out (FIFO).

Immediately, I asked the existing hardlines manager to institute this approach. After about ten days, we were back to an accepted timeline for processing any non-problematic orders. Now that things were under control, I turned my attention to other duties I'd partially neglected and left the area to the assigned manager. Despite having instituted an effective approach, in about two weeks the standard had once again slipped significantly. Since this employee was protected by corporate HR based on their tenure and loyalty, we were able to orchestrate his reassignment to an area that was a better match for his skill set and where he performed well. This encounter helped me learn how an accurate assessment of the challenge helps allocate available resources as effectively as possible.

It's very important to project confidence in a crisis. This self-assurance should be a byproduct of having a well-thought out and clearly documented disaster strategy and reviewing it periodically. If we don't know what to do, it will contribute to our demise. The people we report to will consider replacing us when we no longer have solutions, ideas, or proposals to remedy problems or if we can't at least execute a plan (see: "Respond Quickly").

I would like to add one additional comment that relates to handling a crisis, but also applies to hitting everyday deadlines. Often, when we ask a vendor or a staff member by what date they can accomplish a task, they won't offer the fastest scenario. When the tables turn and our boss seeks the same from us, we probably don't either. *Note: To give you an idea, if my boss asks me to do an analysis, I may request one week to complete the task. However, he may need it for the Board of Directors' meeting in two days.*

If the completion date you're offered is unacceptable because it doesn't keep the project on schedule or meet upper management expectations, you need to negotiate a tighter deadline. If time allows, begin that mediation by explaining the circumstances and timetables to those involved and then pose the question again. If this process isn't getting you anywhere after reasonable effort, you may need to personally mandate the earlier deadline, reinforcing the urgency while asking for your team's support.

REPORTS CAN MISLEAD

Just because it's on a report doesn't mean it's reality. There are many possibilities for how incorrect information shows up. People can unintentionally—or even intentionally—enter inaccurate data, making things look better or worse on everything from statements to resumes. Work in progress (WIP) reports can be wrong because people overlook changing the status of orders when they become problematic, or because contingencies don't exist to capture uncommon occurrences like a carton falling from a conveyor belt. I'm aware of at least one manager who consistently claimed better daily "on standard" performance because of a burning desire to get promoted. Take grocery store barcodes, for example. You might pay a higher price for an item because the stock keeping unit (SKU) didn't have the promotional price entered into the company's database. Have you ever experienced this while watching items being rung up at the register?

One case was a situation where we sent several pallets of product and marketing aids to a grand opening in Canada. All of the freight didn't arrive, and the foul-up caused a lot of embarrassment and frustration on both ends since many VIPs were in attendance. The major third-party fulfillment center swore the lost portion of their shipment wasn't in their warehouse nearest the destination. Six weeks later, the freight finally turned up. The merchandise was later discovered sitting on a partially dismantled—and now unlabeled—pallet in plain sight. During the mishap, on at least three different occasions we asked them to search their facilities, but apparently no one went to the trouble, they just looked at their reports. Their initial response was consistent: blame the independent trucking company for delivering the freight to an incorrect address. We asked for and received compensation beyond our insurance limits, since best operational practices weren't in place at the carrier's facility, including conducting a daily physical inspection of the premises. We lobbied for the facility manager to at least get a severe reprimand. If he didn't get disciplined, he should have.

We can't just manage by being a desk jockey and looking at a piece of paper or listening to a narrative. The opposite, equally myopic approach, would be to park ourselves on the work floor and not examine the documents available. Neither tactic is good enough alone. Yes, we need to look at W.I.P. reports to monitor service standards, alert ourselves to developing trends, and identify red flags (see: "Identify and Monitor Pulse Points"). But we also need to personally observe work-related activity for the same reasons. The reality television series *Undercover Boss* showed how much corporate executives missed until they connected with workers and began surveying conditions for themselves. Sam Walton was a great example of someone who stayed in touch, driving around to stores in his old truck and monitoring circumstances firsthand.

Unacceptably high payroll may be correctly reflected on reports, but calling someone on the phone and chewing them out isn't preventative, diagnostic, or collaborative. A printout does little to tell you if processes are being followed, morale is low, equipment is malfunctioning, and so on.

Allow me to offer another experience of working in a recently remodeled warehouse, where about six million dollars had been spent to place new material handling equipment, which included miles of conveyor belts and new software. One day, a director from another division within the company called me and wanted to know why we had the same trailer in a dock bay for over eight hours. She was looking at a new report on her computer that tracked trailer movement in and out of individual receiving bays (each door was barcoded, as was each company-owned trailer). This long delay was generally unacceptable in an environment where we could receive up to forty trailer deliveries or loads per day and where the goal was to turn shipments around in no more than two hours. The load in question was an "opportunity buy" made by a senior executive, and his aide hadn't completed a purchase order yet. Because this inquiring director wasn't my boss, my somewhat cheeky response ran something to the effect of, "I didn't know that you were involved in overseeing receiving operations, but since you're interested I'll try to answer your question." I went on to explain, "We're not going to handle the freight on this trailer the hard way, which would entail unloading and then spreading the contents out on the warehouse floor, just to manually create an internal purchase order when the details associated with this sale should already exist. If we start doing that, the senior executive's aide will always expect it. The trailer in question is going to sit in the dock until we get a purchase order. If we need the bay, we'll have the hostler (a truck driver in a specialized tractor moving trailers in and out of dock doors) stage the trailer in the yard until we get the appropriate document."

Despite the thought and effort that had gone into the design of the report (a good argument for involving the line managers actually running the area), it didn't gather all of the relevant facts. It should have allowed for coding shipments or adding clarifying comments. Because of this report design oversight, in my absence the director would need to talk to someone on the warehouse floor or physically come and take a look rather than assuming we were asleep at the wheel.

CONTROL THE SITUATION

While conducting interviews, I've periodically presented a hypothetical situation to the applicant. The situation involves a scenario where the candidate is asked to presume that they're the manager over an area. As such, they've decided one of the basic processes in their department needs to change. This decision was reached after consulting with key staff members and gaining upper management's support. There will be significant cost savings by implementing it. Their next step is to bring their department together and announce the new course of action. At this meeting, a couple of negative employees who don't like change begin to resist and question the plan. It becomes obvious after several comments that these two individuals won't welcome the modification no matter how much research or reassurance is given. It's at this point that I pose a question to the applicant: "As the manager, how would you handle this situation?"

Over the years, I've heard a wide variety of responses. A preferred reply would incorporate such thoughts as: (a) after politely responding to a few negative questions, they'd take the conversation offline because it's the manager's meeting, and ultimately they're in charge; (b) employees with their own agendas or detrimental intentions shouldn't be allowed to take control, so in a calm and confident manner the supervisor should inform the department tactfully that the plan to change will proceed on the assigned date; and, (c) arrangements to privately meet with the unhappy employees would be made and held prior to the kickoff date, so an objective discussion about their concerns could occur. This conversation needs to transpire quickly, so disgruntled employees aren't able to try to work up a lot of support among their peers, and this also provides the opportunity to incorporate any valid suggestions the employees offer. Furthermore, these chats should be one-on-one which prevents any possible dissidents from empowering an *ad hoc* group, recognizing a group spokesperson (like a union shop), or putting the manager in a situation where they're outnumbered.

Periodically, there are a few contrary or pessimistic people in a department of any real size. If they're left in the dark (which you should work to avoid), these individuals can become inflammatory and jump to inaccurate conclusions. This is because they don't have the facts themselves, they fear the worst, or they find pleasure in misrepresenting or vilifying your motives and intentions (worst case scenario). Alarmists can have a lot of influence with a group because they're often outspoken. If they begin to stir the pot over an issue, communicate as soon as possible with the natural leaders and positive people to get them on your side (assuming you're acting responsibly and in good faith). Focus next on winning over those who could go one way or the other, to keep them from becoming emotionally charged by more forceful associates (see: "Three Types of Workers"). If they have a stronger relationship with some team members than you do, a disgruntled employee may prevent you from convincing other coworkers that your intentions are admirable. Arm the staff with all of the relevant facts so they won't fall for one-sided, negative characterizations of the matter. If you wait to communicate and disinformation gets out, pessimistic individuals will often misinterpret it. If there's going to be an issue with a portion of the workforce, do everything to pare down the group of skeptics to just a few individuals.

Allow me to restate this in a slightly different manner. By taking control of the situation and educating everyone who is reasonable, you minimize the number of naysayers. Following any other sequence, you may face an uphill battle since negative employees move rapidly to win peer support in the absence of open communication from management. Sharing the facts discredits any malcontents and will take the legitimacy out of any concerns which team members may have or to which they may be exposed. When a skeptic tries to sway them, informed staff members have already evaluated the logic and can counter or dismiss these arguments. Of course, you must be acting in the common good, and your personal credibility also impacts this situation (see: "The Most Important Word"). If you reassured the staff that things would work out previously and they did, the element of trust will serve you well.

Diligently work to establish a culture where team members will seek to clarify facts by following chain of command before seeking information or recourse elsewhere. Combine this with an effective open-door policy where employees can get their questions answered. Conversing logically and honestly with everyone who will listen usually accomplishes this goal. Additionally, utilize common courtesy and kindness while providing straightforward direction, which makes it easier for upper management to support you as you maintain positive control (see: "Ask, Don't Command").

Controlling a situation can take many forms. Let me offer another illustration that may help you handle a difficult circumstance if you face a challenge to your authority. While working in a distribution facility, one morning my boss and mentor told me about an encounter he had with an employee late the afternoon before. They were talking unaccompanied on the warehouse floor when the man decided to register his disgust to a response concerning policy by spitting at the VP's feet. *Note: Before proceeding, this might be a good place for you to ask yourself how you would handle this situation.*

My boss merely offered the employee a choice: he could either go get a paper towel and wipe the floor or be suspended from the premises. My supervisor didn't physically or emotionally react, although the other man was obviously trying to provoke him. He calmly took control on his own terms. Since my mentor was a linebacker in college, he could have physically asserted himself, but ultimately, he would have been the biggest loser for choosing that response. Pretending that nothing had happened would have been a victory for the employee, since he could get away with unacceptable conduct. This might empower other recalcitrant employees as well.

In my opinion, the situation was handled correctly. The employee decided he needed his job and my boss waited while he retrieved a paper towel from the restroom. It ended calmly without the need to say much more or to take corrective action (which would have been an excessive measure as this was his first violation). My boss knew what actions his authority entitled him to utilize when a belligerent employee challenged him, while not blowing the situation out of proportion.

While working at the same center, my boss and I had an experience involving a supervisor who ran the ready-to-wear (RTW) or goods-on-hangers (GOH) department. This area processed clothing that either arrived on or needed hangers inserted. We were implementing a new incentive plan and replacing an old one disliked by virtually all of the staff. To avoid repeating that problem, we wanted the employees to be involved in tailoring the new program to fairly account for the broad array of work they performed. We used this approach because a program will be more readily accepted if you give significant formative input to those impacted. To help achieve this goal, each department selected two representatives to advocate their coworkers' interests and concerns at weekly meetings with senior leadership and the consultants overseeing the effort. These representatives would discuss issues and then go back and share the outcomes and decisions with their colleagues, so they didn't feel like new standards were being shoved down their throats.

One day, when one of these meetings was to be held, the supervisor mentioned didn't send his delegates. When I went out on the warehouse floor to remind him, he curtly responded, "I'm not sending them, we're too busy." My measured response was, "I realize you're busy, but we can authorize overtime or I can get some people from another area to help tomorrow." This didn't persuade him to send the representatives. I asked again with no luck. The third time I said, "You don't understand—I'm trying to ask nicely, but this is a request I expect you to support. We need these people at the meeting, so the new incentive program will become what everyone wants" (see: "Ask, Don't Command"). When he refused a fourth time, I said, "If you won't send them, then I'll find it necessary to suspend you." The supervisor responded, "If you suspend me, then I'm not going to leave." I countered, "That's fine, if you understand that you're not on the clock and that you can't become disruptive. If you do, I'll find it necessary for you to leave or be removed from the premises." While I accompanied his representatives to the meeting, he called an executive in a nearby building and requested an audience. Because our ultimate boss had an open-door policy and was a compassionate individual, he obliged. During their phone conversation, the supervisor told the executive that he felt threatened, so the senior manager sent someone to pick him up.

Afterward, my boss had a conversation with this executive so he could understand the situation from all sides (see: "The Most Important Word"). This was followed a day or two later by a small meeting with a few key members of the management team, including the defiant supervisor. The senior manager personally attended and was kind, thanking the supervisor and others for their loyalty over the years, but he reinforced that the program needed to move forward.

This supervisor had used up his favor (see: "Spend Goodwill, but Carefully"). As people usually do in this situation, he realized he couldn't keep asking the executive to intervene on his behalf, especially when he was being unreasonable. The moral of this story is to be careful when you call in a marker like this since you can't do it more than once or twice. A superior may appreciate you and see you as valuable, but repeated occurrences of this significance will likely become an annoyance and get you labeled as difficult. Frequently, such an individual won't make more than a couple of requests for intervention, because they perceive their goodwill account is empty (see: "Seek Respect Before Friendship").

TWO STRIKES ALLOWED

At several places where I've worked, we applied a "Two Strike Rule." In effect, it means that everyone gets just two chances to address most issues before the other party moves the request up the corporate ladder or chain of command. This applies to simple things like getting a signature on a time-off request to more important matters like getting an exceptional accommodation in response to a problem involving a customer. Critical issues don't apply, nor do they merit the latitude of two strikes.

To illustrate: if you needed a coworker to confirm the accuracy of some verbiage in a change of policy letter going to your customers, you would only need to ask them twice. The second request might be something like, "I know you're busy, but I asked you two days ago to look this over. If you can't give me your changes by the end of today, I'll need to ask your manager to review it tomorrow morning because that's the deadline." As covered earlier, you can even invite them to go with you to the boss if there's a disagreement about how to handle things. If they try and play the friendship or sympathy card, you need to respond, "Yes, I consider you a friend, but that doesn't mean I'm willing to neglect my duties because you won't find time to work this into your schedule" (see: "Spend Goodwill, but Carefully" and "Seek Respect Before Friendship").

If one of your team members is dealing with someone outside of your division and has been accused of being unsupportive when applying this approach, train them to explain that their supervisor (meaning, us) insists that matters go up the chain of command after two attempts. They can further clarify that if they don't escalate the assignment, they're in violation of a division rule. Since they're accountable to their department head, this trumps the complainant's request to give them extra time to fulfill their portion of the task. This also provides them with a legitimate excuse for being somewhat unsympathetic to a peer's selfish plea. This should tactfully convey the message that if they're trying to buy themselves some slack at a peer's expense, they better find another candidate.

IDENTIFY AND MONITOR PULSE POINTS

Have you ever swept water on a flat surface? When you sweep on just one side, a lot of the water on the other side runs back to fill the area where you just swept. This can serve as an analogy for overseeing a work unit. Don't leave part of your responsibilities to chance. If you focus on some details at the exclusion of others—including the bigger picture—sooner or later something will resist improvement efforts. An example might be a construction superintendent putting in extra electrical outlets while subcontractors fall behind schedule waiting for them to provide clarification detail on their awarded work.

We need to establish a disciplined approach by which our team should operate along with a systemic methodology for monitoring key performance measures. Since we can't anticipate every possibility, and some incidents are too minor to merit a contingency plan, what saves us in these situations is the ability to identify difficulties or glitches early on and to react swiftly and intelligently. Just as gauges in our car warn that the gas is low before we're stranded miles from a service station, or that the oil is low before we burn up an engine, information is needed that helps systematically evaluate critical activities or relevant indicators regarding our responsibilities. Without this in place, we'll find ourselves either making very little progress or frantically moving back and forth to wherever the need seems to be greatest at that moment, like sweeping water.

In a manufacturing environment, we must know how many units to produce each day, which is known as a production capacity plan and which includes resources like the manpower, consumables or raw materials, and equipment speed necessary to achieve that result. Likewise, we need to examine sales results and work orders to know if demand has changed. If we only monitor these indicators every few days, it will be too late to avoid serious complications. However, if we identify at the start of the day or during regular daily rounds that the workload has increased or that resources are insufficient to satisfy revised weekly production demand for the upcoming week, we can react swiftly and avoid catastrophe. It takes time to call in more labor, switch over equipment, and find and stage additional raw materials. If we take definitive action as soon as indicators suggest, we're better off than allowing the difficulty to grow unchecked into something so big that minor corrections can't fix it.

I offer this advice because I've witnessed managers behind on service standards who did too little or nothing to correct the problem, hoping to get a break or lull in workload. This is an ill-advised approach. To illustrate, if on Tuesday you're a day behind on production and full staff working on Saturday could get the department current, why wouldn't you choose to schedule overtime—you could cancel later if necessary—instead of entering the next week already behind the standard for service (see: "Controlling and Utilizing Overtime")? If you bring yourself current with whatever working hours are available for the remainder of the week, you can then respond more effectively to new challenges you encounter. But if you choose to solve the negative situation next week by working overtime then, you'll be at a serious disadvantage when dealing with new complications that arise. By the way, who has better standing: the team who is behind for a day or two or the team who is behind every day for a week or longer (see: "The Most Important Word")? Approximately the same amount of overtime is used, but which tactic also better serves customer service?

Take time to identify all of the key metrics and indicators and then determine the best manner to assess them. If you're new to the organization, be sure to get the input of team members; inevitably, you'll overlook measures that should have been on your radar and then you'll have to pay the price for missing them. Let me also warn again that it's impossible to effectively run an operation off reports or just from an ivory tower office. Sometimes, reports include incorrect data (see: "Reports can Mislead"). Regularly confirm if all is well with your own two eyes. Remember to go about inspections purposely, looking for seemingly inconspicuous signs. Try to observe whatever you may not normally notice (like the billboard on the way to work you can't recall). This reminds me of a housekeeping manager who always looked down at his shoes whenever he walked around the facility. "He does that so he doesn't have to see what needs to be cleaned," our boss would moan.

Accept the reality that employees may not act the same in our presence—especially if we occupy a prominent role—as they do when they think we're not around. Try walking away from a group and then turn around to observe them after they think you're safely out of sight. On occasion, you'll be surprised to see people sit down or start engaging in horseplay. An old GEICO commercial joked, "If your boss stops by, you act like you're working. It's what you do."[22]

If you have managers reporting to you that oversee departments or major functions, in addition to regular walkthroughs I suggest you require monthly status reports from these managers as part of your approach. This is a great tool to stay abreast of progress and for addressing issues which have been neglected or forgotten. This is an application of the principle "inspect what you expect." Although this isn't as good as fixing problems immediately, it's better than letting them spread.

Checklists—prioritized by task and requiring a response—are a valuable communication tool for staff that may be working different shifts or with whom we don't have regular interaction opportunities. Checklists help ensure that "the water gets to the end of the row," meaning that everyone who needs to know is informed, consequently eliminating misunderstandings and excuse-making. Staff members and teams need to be assigned a workload that matches or slightly exceeds the amount of time it will take them to complete if they work steadily, allowing for the reality that some tasks are accomplished more quickly than anticipated (see: "Set Higher Standards"). This facilitates the achievement of planned output and provides staff members with a sense of accomplishment associated with appropriate effort. Include notification alerts like phone calls or texts for serious events, and writing up shift notes for less critical occurrences. Compliment teams and individuals who can be relied upon to fulfill these assignments.

Note: When tracking output, you'll sometimes need a blended UPH (units per hour) measurement. To illustrate, some operations may only track shipped

---

[22] "10 Funniest GEICO It's What You Do Commercials.mp4." *YouTube*, uploaded by Fun House 64, 23 Sept. 2016, youtube.com/watch?v=U9vfT7tjrmY. Accessed 11 April 2023.

units, but how will they explain if hours are up due to heavy inbound receipts when shipped units are flat or below planned levels? This also pertains to sales departments with lighter than expected cold calls, but higher referrals which haven't yet turned into sales dollars. In several warehouses and distribution centers I've overseen, it was necessary to track units shipped as well as orders shipped. This was because the customary ratio between the two was periodically abnormal. To show you what I mean, the average units per order may have been around five items, but during a sales event the units could blossom to nine or more. Former tracking metrics may reflect fewer or similar order quantities during the period, but this wouldn't account for the significant increase in total workload resulting from the spike in the units per order. Nor would it help justify the extra fulfillment labor scheduled during the sale.

To recap: be predictable in what you require of teams. The current phrase we hear to describe this is "transparency." Continuity is an important part of a work culture and has value in a creative setting although the boundaries are much broader. Effort and progress are wasted when people have to try to figure out what their boss wants. Once you've determined your pulse points, communicate them.

CONTROLLING AND UTILIZING OVERTIME

There's a small percentage of employees who, if unmonitored, will stay longer than scheduled on certain days to increase their paychecks. To avoid this, supplemental hours and pay should be approved in advance by someone in management who understands the associated costs and issues. Time and time again, I've seen situations where the overtime (OT) hours—costing one-and-a-half times the standard hourly rate—didn't result in the productivity gains experienced during regular hours. *Note: For a supervisory position requiring preparation for shift start-up and wrap-up, establish a reasonable, yet fixed, time allowance for those duties, perhaps fifteen to thirty minutes before and after the shift. To save some of that expense in start-up operations, any supervisors could be scheduled for an hour lunch, rather than thirty minutes, with leads covering the time gap.*

The first effort in managing overtime is to shut off any of it that's not approved daily, and then see what isn't getting done. Since we'll inevitably experience some creep with regard to unapproved hours worked, one approach other than not paying overtime (not endorsed since it's illegal) is to have our supervisory staff monitor it daily. They can then direct offending employees to take longer lunches or leave early on subsequent days during that same pay period, until the excess time is eliminated.

Don't fall prey to the person who frequently asks you to approve their timesheet because they supposedly forgot to clock in. Most likely they were late and want to avoid the consequences, which include less pay and being subjected to performance coaching. The best way to handle this is to say, "I'll enter the shift start time for you today but going forward I'll use the actual time when you bring the issue to me. Part of your job is to remember to clock in."

The next step is to ascertain if you're maximizing your most impactful resources, including machinery. Too often managers request additional capital expenditures or extended work shifts rather than figuring out how to leverage what they already have. One department comes to mind. They kept buying more equipment, remodeling their workspace, and approving OT when another solution was available. The operation was a short drive from an outstanding university with many students who would have loved a decent paying afternoon or evening part-time job related to their major. The addition of a partial second shift would have improved the department's throughput and service performance considerably while saving literally hundreds of thousands of dollars.

Third, if the area isn't composed of production line staff, have the supervisor provide a list of the daily, weekly, and monthly tasks each coworker is expected to accomplish and how long each assignment should take (don't disclose that you're looking at overtime). If the workload truly requires more than 40 hours a week, you now have data in hand to facilitate simplifying, eliminating, or reassigning a portion of these duties.

Finally, hiring another employee is the last consideration after you've explored alternatives first. If the spike in volume reflects a condition that is small and short-lived, then it's less expensive to have trained staff work additional hours. This is because it's cheaper to pay an existing team member the bonus rate when they can produce greater output than a temporary worker. To illustrate, paying $35.00 an hour to cover the expense of a regular employee who has been with you a year ($20.00/hour multiplied by 1.5 equals $30.00, plus 25% of the base rate or $5.00 to cover benefits) to produce 100 units per hour equals $0.35 per unit. A temporary worker might cost $23.40 an hour ($18.00/hour multiplied by 1.3 to cover a 30% agency mark-up) and initially produce only 50 units. Add to that $8.33 an hour ($25.00 divided by three) for a trainer on benefits to oversee three trainees and you're at $31.73, pushing the trainees' cost per unit up to $0.635 per item processed. That's almost double the expense. Of course, they become more efficient over time, but you're examining a short-term need. *Note: These numbers were chosen not to indicate what you should pay, but rather to keep the example simple.*

	Hourly Expense	Units Per Hour	Cost Per Unit
Seasoned Staff Member on Overtime	$30.00	100	$0.300
Benefit Cost for Seasoned Employee	$5.00	100	$0.050
TOTAL: Seasoned Employee Costs	**$35.00**	**100**	**$0.350**
Temp Employee with Fee (w/o OT)	$23.40	50	$0.468
Training Cost for Temp Employee	$8.33	50	$0.167
TOTAL: Temp Employee Costs	**$31.73**	**50**	**$0.635**

If you perform these preventative measures and still see more than 25 hours/week in overtime (the equivalent of 37.5 hours in payroll) and believe the increase in workload will sustain or increase over the coming months, hire and train a new team member as soon as possible. On a larger scale, if you have 24 team members all working effectively and efficiently and logging ten hours of bonus pay per week, that's 240 hours (the payroll equivalent of 360 hours). Hire at least six additional people (or more if you project the trend to continue) who'll be able to cover those 240 hours once they're up to speed. Remember that new hires will lower the production of any trainers and take several weeks or months to reach standard productivity. If you expect the workload volume to drop off, bring people in as seasonal employees so in fairness they understand that they may work reduced hours or could be laid off.

Bringing in seasonal or temporary employees isn't my first preference, but there are situations when they may be the best option. This would include witnessing a significant spike in volume which may not last and which you can't successfully handle with a reasonable amount of overtime. Sources for part-time staff might include workers in non-competing professions, students, and homemakers (male and female) who are looking for supplemental income. The downside includes the possibility that they aren't seeking a long-term job. Payroll must absorb the repeating cost of training seasonal workers, since you're apt to lose them more frequently than regular new hires. Temporary staff members rarely have the same emotional tie to the company as a long-time employee. The expenses of poorer accuracy and potential damage to customer goodwill can also be associated with this as they learn the ropes.

I must admit, one benefit is being able to evaluate a temporary worker and let them go at the first sign they're a poor match. *Note: In contrast to managing temporary employees, experience has shown that most firms benefit from conducting several performance coaching sessions with newly-hired regular employees even though they're still in a probationary period.*

Negotiate the agency fee down as low as possible without jeopardizing the company's commitment to your account. A temporary staffing firm's normal way to charge involves adding an additional percentage on top of the hourly rate. As calculated earlier, imagine paying $18.00 an hour with a fee of 30%. That converts to $23.40 an hour. You can get the fee as low as 25% to 30% if the service supplies you with many employees because they experience some economies in hiring, screening, and so forth. Factor in how much extraordinary prescreening or training you require since this increases an agency's overhead. Don't expect the lowest agency fees if you're requesting just a few workers each month. Be careful not to insist on a margin so low (usually under 25%) that the provider can't perform their services satisfactorily or they'll give preferential treatment to another customer.

Make the starting base rate for temporary employees the same as new regular employees in each specific position. That wage should be equal to—if not slightly higher than—the competition's. This prevents losing them to better compensation elsewhere. If not, other firms using temp services in your area can easily make you the candidates' last choice whenever they have assignment options. You may get exactly what you've paid for. Moreover, avoid losing a capable temp employee while waiting to convert them to long-term staff by communicating that there are permanent positions openings with a raise available (the equivalent of a 90-day evaluation) if they keep up the good work. Attractive benefits when they transition and additional increase opportunities at six months and annually (from their start date as a temporary worker) should be part of your company's approach and are worth mentioning.

Most agencies charge a lump sum to convert temporary employees to staff (often a percentage of the individual's potential earnings if they make it sixty or ninety days, which can become hundreds or thousands of dollars with multiple conversions). Reach a reasonable agreement as to when you can make this transition, perhaps as early as two months, with a suitable candidate without incurring a charge. My recommendation is to avoid paying a fee to convert qualified temps to long-term staff earlier than this agreed-upon period since you never know when they might take another job, go back to school, decide to move out of state, or something similar. In these situations, the fee is wasted.

Along these lines, don't panic when one of your supervisors exclaims, "I need more help." Proactively substantiate the facts surrounding the need. I recall a situation where part of the duties of one of my quality assurance departments was assigned to another division. There were four staff members in the original department. Two moved to the new department, while two stayed. About three years later, the new group had grown to six while the smaller original department still accomplished their tasks successfully with two. The manager overseeing our small group—along with other areas—received occasional complaints from her team stating they'd witnessed employees from the larger spin-off department killing time unproductively and overheard two of them talking about how they filled their day with tasks unrelated to the job. Beware of supervisors or managers who want or build a small empire or have excess resources solely to handle a rare emergency.

Allow me to cover a couple of related topics. Before having trainees work overtime, consider whether they've reached an acceptable production level. Poor performers should be coached into standard performance levels or into an employment opportunity elsewhere. Under-producing team members love working bonus hours, and getting rewarded for their unacceptable work behaviors (see: "Three Types of Workers"). The flip side is that they may prefer to stay home every chance they get, but if you exclude them from scheduled overtime this sends the wrong message to productive staff members who wanted the day off.

Work out how to handle this dilemma with other members of the management team. This provides further reason to deal with employees' work-related faults or substandard performance in a timely manner.

If someone misses an extra shift, it's an attendance infraction and I've even seen it count as a double violation (this must be a written policy beforehand).

Another suggestion is to consider establishing mandatory overtime, especially when you can't get enough volunteers to meet business needs. *Note: Well-liked managers generally get a better response to recruiting for additional hours than their counterparts. However, if the operation is continually relying on overtime because hiring efforts are lagging behind the projected need, even these managers will experience difficulties getting an adequate response when compliance is voluntary.* If you adopt this policy, it should be covered in the orientation manual. Allow exceptions for legitimate issues like weddings, funerals, or even to watch their child perform in a tournament. To be considerate, announce when extra work hours will be put into play as early as possible. Consider how you would feel to find out on a Thursday or Friday that you're working on Saturday when you already had plans. Perhaps giving each regular employee (those no longer on a typical 90-day introductory period) a small number of passes annually will help buffer their frustrations. These passes should be available for use when they have a conflict for a previously unscheduled weekend shift.

As a general observation, due to fatigue anything beyond ten hours of work per day is a waste of payroll unless you're in an unusual crisis. If you must schedule overtime, try to create incentive for staff to leave early if they accomplish the workload earlier than expected. For example, "We're scheduled to work eight hours on Saturday, but we can leave before that if we fill the 5,000 orders sooner." In this scenario, more time with family or friends might sufficiently motivate crews so you don't need to pay more OT than necessary.

In a related vein, when you transition a staff member from hourly status to a salary position (non-exempt versus exempt), look at how much overtime they earned over the last twelve months when establishing their new salary. Make it clear that you expect a minimum of 45 to 48 hours per week and sometimes a lot more when things are hopping. Hopefully there has been some thoughtful control of the worker's bonus earnings, so they weren't making more as an hourly employee than they would in management. If this isn't the case, they may not want the promotion because they'd be taking a pay cut. If this happens, your first action should be to eliminate their supplemental hours or at least get them back to a reasonable level. Then down the road they may find the salaried position more attractive.

ORDER SERVES SUCCESS

A simple illustration supports my belief that doing things incorrectly often takes more time and effort than doing them the right way. An industrial engineer doing time and motion studies on the act of disposing trash should confirm that it takes less total effort for employees to throw waste in conveniently placed containers rather than having a custodian clean up the garbage they dropped on the floor. Disposing of refuse correctly requires less time because there is less handling (fewer touches involved). Touching something once—assessing what action the item merits and performing that task now without procrastinating—applies to many activities we find ourselves doing including processing mail (snail and electronic). Expanding this logic, it's less expensive and easier to maintain a physical space in presentable and operational order than it is to get it back into that condition after gross neglect.

One of my employers had offices in an 80-year-old building located in Oregon. Everyone eventually vacated that space for a newer corporate facility, except for a production operation which was left in one section. The rest of the deteriorating building was cluttered with all of the equipment, furniture, irrelevant records, worthless office supplies, and trash that should have been disposed of prior to the move. More than once, we said it looked like someone yelled "Fire!" and everyone threw their work up in the air and ran out, never to return. Among other items left in the building were uninstalled odd-colored plumbing fixtures, the origin of which I never learned. Apparently, staff in a variety of departments (maintenance, custodial, and IT, to name a few) felt we might need it someday. Would you purposely use extremely outdated and mismatched items in any actively-operating corporate office where image was important? There were carpet remnants too small for patch jobs, exercise equipment beyond repair, obsolete personal computers and fax machines, and buckets of screws, bolts, and nails mixed together (it would take longer to find what you need than it would to go buy more).

On a smaller scale, I'm reminded of a maintenance worker in Pennsylvania who tried to be very frugal with the company's money. He would get in his car, drive sixty miles roundtrip, and take nearly 90 minutes to retrieve a tool or part he needed from another facility. This process was often repeated, despite pleas from his manager to buy the necessary supplies or equipment required at each location. Moreover, if he needed an inexpensive part for a common repair, he would go to the store and buy just one instead of getting extras.

A coworker shared with me an excerpt from a book called *The Value of Order* by Harry Myers. One of the points the book makes is that hanging onto things you don't need or rarely use is costly when you compare the effort of storing, relocating, and finding these items.[23] On a large scale, having scores of pallet spaces in the racking full of items that are no longer selling (over-inventoried, out of style, past shelf life, shop worn, etc.) can be very costly. On occasion to help us make a point with senior management and/or the buyer over a category, we calculated the annual storage cost of one pallet space. The intent was to help them decide the best financial and responsible course of action, for example lowering the price, donating the merchandise, or as last resort recycling or disposing of the products

---

[23] Myers, Harry. *The Value of Order*. E. H. Tingley, 1942. pp. 5-14.

in question. The expense calculation could include rent per square foot, utilities, labor, and even the cost of warehousing viable inventory in a supplemental lease space.

A friend of mine worked in an environment where they were trained to use the 5S methodology. While I'm not thoroughly acquainted with the approach, I'm offering an overview because I agree with its ideology. 5S is a system for handling workplace organization and stands for Sort, Set in Order, Shine, Standardize, and Sustain. This system involves going through everything in a space, deciding what is necessary (a very important step), putting items in order, cleaning, and setting up procedures for repeating the process on a regular basis (not just a one-time event). This methodology is often thought of as foundational to "lean manufacturing" since orderly workplaces seek to reduce waste and increase efficiency. Hence, tools and materials are placed in logical locations based on who needs them and how often they're utilized.[24]

Somewhat related is "Kaizen," a lean manufacturing concept that refers to the ongoing effort of finding ways to enhance processes over time. For it to work well, everyone in the workplace participates by looking for how tasks can be improved. 5S sets up a workplace to also use Kaizen. Once a 5S organizational system exists, people can more easily look for value-added opportunities.[25]

Truly, organization and simplicity are the best framework and approach. The cost associated with getting organized and remaining that way from day one is less than the ongoing expense of operating in a condition of disarray.

---

[24] "What is 5s?" *5SToday*, 2023, 5stoday.com/what-is-5s/. Accessed 3 March 2023.

[25] "Kaizen." *LeanProduction*, 2023, leanproduction.com/kaizen/. Accessed 3 March 2023.

RESEARCH REOCCURRING PROBLEMS TO THE INDIVIDUAL

I'm sure by now you've noticed the concepts in this book aren't rocket science. Nevertheless, straightforward ideas aren't always adopted as readily as we would hope. One of my bosses used to say, "There are no miracles. The only real miracle is the application of common sense." Maybe this can help us understand why people sit in a seminar and agree with the viewpoints being taught, but then go back to work not realizing they're failing to employ the very principles they just decided to adopt. Why that happens is anybody's guess. Do people just return to old habits, are they oblivious, or what? Whatever the case, it's clearly human nature to often assume the other person is the one who should make all of the improvements. If you're reading this book, you are part of the population who wants to look at matters objectively and then self-correct as needed.

If a work unit is experiencing a problem, the first objective is to identify the cause and correct it. After the challenge is overcome, you may need to get to the bottom of the issue because the failure was too flagrant to remain unaddressed. It's now time to research the matter down to the individual(s) (see: "The Blame Game").

Once it's been determined whose actions resulted in the performance failure, what course of action is best? If you're in a management role and you stand up and say, "Someone is manufacturing faulty product," or, "Individuals are turning in reports with inaccurate data," almost everybody in the room will assume you're talking about someone else and that they're not guilty. If they do realize it's them, they might hope you haven't figured that out yet. Otherwise, why is a meeting being held with the entire department (see: "Establishing Accountability")? Generally, this group approach is inappropriate because a negative subject was discussed with the whole team, but most of them aren't guilty. This has also been characterized as "preaching to the choir." If you're innocent and regularly subjected to this approach, it gets old quickly. Expanding on this, all of the conscientious employees who follow processes and try to give their best effort could easily take offense. One of the worst things you can do is wrongfully accuse someone. Insinuating that they may have a problem is only slightly less egregious.

On the other hand, when you track a serious mistake back to the specific person responsible, they're usually surprised when you sit down with them privately (see: "Micromanage Non-Performers"). Suddenly, the lights go on, it becomes very personal and meaningful, so they pay attention when you inform them that the situation was thoroughly researched and it's confirmed they were at fault. *Warning: If you feel the need to pull the team together to discuss this issue from a training perspective, do your best to keep it positive.*

To make sure you handle the conversation with the offending employee fittingly, factor in their intent and how often this event has occurred. Unless it was unpardonable, performance coaching is in order. Keep in mind that it's difficult for people expending a lot of energy at work to be criticized, since they can't easily differentiate between effort and effectiveness. If this is the case, help them understand that the issue isn't how vigorously they're engaged. Rather, you need them to be more effective which may help them feel less overwhelmed (see: "Overwhelming To-Do Lists").

WHY CREATE A REPORT?

At one distribution center where I worked, we sent out a trailer-load of goods to almost all of the thirty stores each day of the work week. Once a trailer filled, a driver would move it full of new merchandise to the dock of the designated store. They would then hook up their tractor to an empty trailer already stationed at the store. That trailer had been emptied of previously-delivered new merchandise by store personnel and prepared for return by being partially reloaded with transfers to other stores, empty

CONCEPTS OF MANAGING

freight bins, and old appliances or mattresses coming from delivery of furniture to customers' homes. Upon arrival back at the warehouse, these returning trailers needed to be unloaded of this odd assortment so they were available to be spotted into a loading dock bay and loaded with merchandise once again. Then the process would repeat itself.

There were a certain number of trailers allotted for this cycle. At any given time during operations, thirty trailers were being loaded at the distribution center for outbound delivery to stores. At least in concept, an additional thirty trailers were usually on the highway moving to or from either location. Another thirty trailers were spotted at the store docks for unloading or partial reloading, with transfers to other stores or junk appliances/furniture returning to the center. This made for a minimum of ninety trailers in circulation. If the staff at the distribution center was slow clearing the returned trailers of transfers and items for disposal, it created a shortage of empty trailers to sustain the shipping process. The hostler (see definition in "Reports can Mislead") wouldn't have enough empty trailers to stage in shipping doors for new outbound store freight. This would create a bottleneck and inefficiencies throughout the process.

When it became a periodic problem, the transportation director would bring this issue up at our morning staff meeting. Correcting the matter was a nuisance because my staff often had more work than they could complete in a timely basis. Inbound receipts might be heavier than expected, staff members could be sick, or extra effort might be required to prepare a problematic shipment of merchandise. Of course, I was always annoyed and wondered why the director waited to air this topic in front of others—especially our boss—at coordination meetings. Why couldn't he have told me earlier in private (see: "Create Bridges, Not Enemies")? On the other hand, he was understandably frustrated by our inability to monitor this by ourselves, so he created a report.

At first, the creation of this new report felt underhanded. Slowly, I came to accept the necessary reality of having the details divulged each morning at staff meeting. After all, we did have 24 hours to make certain there were enough empty trailers to handle our needs for the following day. This became a higher priority once the report was circulated each morning. Months later, I'd accepted the creation of the document and acknowledged the inevitable. The report had accomplished much of what the transportation director had intended.

On occasion I've chosen to implement this approach, to publish information related to another department's performance when it impacted an area for which I was accountable. If the concern had been discussed more than a few times and they still weren't executing at the level required, we created a scorecard for the activity and distributed it at appropriate intervals (see: "Spend Goodwill, but Carefully" and "Two Strikes Allowed"). This way it wouldn't be as easily overlooked and was less of a personal affront than it would be to periodically bring up the matter unannounced. To make this type of report even more palatable and helpful, consider broadening its scope to include dashboard-type metrics from your own area of responsibility. I recommend considering this approach if you're encountering a similar challenge.

MICROMANAGE NON-PERFORMERS

During the middle of my career when interviewing with a national business, I was flown to Colorado to go through a full-day assessment. The company utilized some evaluation tools like those I was exposed to in graduate school. The appraisal included an in-box scenario in which you're supposedly back in your office for just one day before leaving town again. The set-up dictated you had one hour to read your mail and respond to any correspondence you saw fit. The exercise gauged how you prioritized and delegated. Another part of the day was dedicated to responding to written questions about how you would handle various situations. One of the more interesting experiences was being placed in a small meeting with other candidates to see how effective you were in teamwork and accomplishing business goals in meetings.

Although the formal feedback came a week or so later, we spent time at the end of the interview with evaluators as they explored the reasoning behind our actions. One of the questions posed to me concerned why I spent more time with non-performers and micro-managed them, but not as much time with more productive colleagues.

Even now, I find myself handling staff I work with in the same manner. This is likely because I regard myself as an above-average achiever—as most of us view ourselves—and prefer not being micro-managed. Tell me the project goals and their priority along with any cautions and guidelines, permit questions, and then allow me to get on with it. It's okay to request progress reports along the way and to offer advice or redirect me if necessary, but don't look over my shoulder continually and second-guess every minor move I make. Isn't that how all solid achievers feel?

Conversely, there are individuals with a reputation for being non-performers. These employees can't be trusted to work solo because they haven't accomplished the projects they've been entrusted with in the past (see: "Three Types of Workers"). The reasons for this can be as diverse as the individuals: they may have no sense of urgency, they may not like working under somebody else, or their social skills may be so poor they can't engage with others. Trying to work with these individuals is especially difficult if they're peers, they work in another department, or if it isn't apparent their boss is striving to address these behaviors. When they report directly to you, more options become available.

When members of my appointed area forget or neglect their duties, in frustration I wonder why I must remind them of their assignments while also performing my own responsibilities (even though I realize I should be keeping track of their projects). Supervisors need workers who get things done. Managers need people who accept responsibility, run with the ball, and complete tasks on or near schedule. If productive employees need clarification, they ask for it. If they need assistance, they get others to help.

If you have somebody in your department who isn't finishing their assignments either because they forget them or don't want to do them, the rest of your team expects you to deal with this issue because of the negative impact it can have (see: "Everyone Doing Their Share"). Whenever a poor employee is involved in the work equation, their peers must shoulder more of the burden to achieve group objectives. Eventually, a portion of their coworkers start to wonder why they should go above and beyond their duties to make up for the gap in productivity (see: "Three Types of Workers"). Are they giving more because you tolerate substandard efforts from others?

Keep a file on each individual who directly reports to you and include specific details on positive and negative performance. The incidents can be stored on your smartphone, computer, or paper files, but they should contain the facts and include dates. Somewhere along the line I heard these notations referred to as "fat files" because when the folder (electronic or not) starts to grow, it tells you special recognition or discipline is in order.

Unless the conduct is flagrant, engage the person in a private discussion before you issue corrective action or a personal improvement program. Many more wayward comrades get turned around by these off-the-record conversations (sometimes called being "taken behind the woodshed") than anything else. If you're candid and forthright, employees often appreciate the chance to fix things without something going in their official personnel file (different from the "fat file"). If they choose not to mend their ways, they can't profess surprise when you take more formal steps to correct their behavior.

If we micro-manage below-average workers, it puts us in a prime position to evaluate their attitude and skills while either coaching them into line, or if necessary, out the door. Meanwhile, the rest of our department can see we don't accept mediocrity and they consequently stay on task. Of course, keep disciplinary conversations private, but direct involvement in problematic issues signals to the rest of the group that these affairs haven't gone unnoticed. Ultimately, the staff will notice the problem dissipating, their peer's performance improving, or learn of any terminations, transfers, or demotions.

Team environments come with their own unique challenges. There needs to be a clear delineation of responsibilities and accountability. Don't let non-performers hide under the guise of being just another cog in the wheel. They need to attend cross-functional meetings and hit assigned deadlines.

When the facts are in on an unsatisfactory employee, act decisively even if you can't carry out the reprimand or penalty initially recommended (see: "Establishing Accountability"). It's certain that if someone on our workforce isn't doing their part and it's not being addressed, it reflects negatively on the unit and us as well (see: "The Most Important Word"). Perhaps the employee needs additional training. If they do, it needs to be completed over a reasonable amount of time; you can't send them off to get a four-year bachelor's degree. Maybe they can be placed in a less-demanding role. In rare cases this may mean a reduction in pay, but that action only works if the employee sees their deficiencies and wants to either relieve pressure or have time to hone their skills (see: "Establishing Accountability"). It's much easier to let someone go if your employer has a reasonable severance pay policy so they have time to find another position that's a better match.

Managing talent is one of the most difficult aspects of the job—especially for managers who are compassionate—yet it's critical to the success of any venture. We need teams composed of individuals who are self-actualized and have the skills to perform their jobs at the highest level.

EVERYONE DOING THEIR SHARE

While functioning as the manager for a retail anchor store, my entire staff was asked to complete an employee opinion survey about how the unit was run. The responses were tallied by human resources that in turn shared them up the chain of command and with each store's management team. Respondents were protected by anonymity and the company tried to administer these surveys every year. The survey consisted of fifty-four questions organized into nine categories covering clarity, standards, teamwork, initiative, involvement, recognition, concern for employees, compensation/benefits, and quality of service. To say this evaluation made me paranoid is an overstatement, but I was concerned about the results. Other more experienced store managers had given me a head's-up that if you failed the first survey (anything less than a 70% positive score overall), a follow-up appraisal would be given again in three to six months. If the score was still less than 70%, you would be dismissed.

We passed. The overall positive responses were in the low eighties, which allowed me to breathe again. Having lived through the experience, I worked to receive subsequently higher scores so I would never need to go through that pressure again. In reviewing the findings with my district manager, it was good to hear where scores were above average, but some of the negative responses surprised me. One clear theme emerged: namely, that I was too patient with non-performers. The unfiltered message I interpreted from the team's replies was, "We're tired of shouldering the workload of unproductive associates and we want management to ensure they carry their fair share of the burden." As an example, if two clerks scheduled during an evening shift spent it chatting when they were supposed to be recovering the men's department or processing new merchandise receipts, the team members working the next morning had to double their efforts. Similarly, if there was a sale breaking tomorrow and an employee in the housewares area called off just before their shift was to begin—just like they'd done several times previously—this left the remaining employees running themselves ragged trying to set up the ad while assisting customers. This latter example was a pattern for one particular employee and it didn't allow management time to find a replacement.

Previously, my approach had been to go out of the way to communicate with and coach poor performers, giving them corrective actions hesitantly. I thought their peers wanted me to handle them with kid gloves. The feedback from the other survey respondents suggested otherwise. In my own words, they effectively said, "We're tired of compensating for lazy coworkers." Most of the staff didn't want me to go easy on their associates because they wanted consistent, fair treatment. This experience stayed with me and allowed me to be more direct when addressing unmotivated individuals. This proactive approach while still following due process is prudent since it makes a point of looking out for the hard-working members of your team. After all, who would you miss most?

Later, I created my own survey focused primarily on logistics (134 questions) and have used it in the last three companies in which I've worked. If I can create a survey, then surely you can as well. It can be a great tool if your boss or an unhappy employee who takes it upon themself to speak up for others, comments that morale is in the tank.

One time after giving the survey on our own and sharing the results, my boss's supervisor wanted to go through the survey line by line and discuss the responses. We accommodated and humored her, but I wanted to say, "Wouldn't your time be better spent with the division heads who have never solicited feedback from their staff? Don't worry about us because we're actually trying to improve performance."

Regarding the process, after administering any survey and then computing the results, division leadership should hold meetings and give a broad overview of results that pertain to the work unit polled. This includes requests for improvements to the facility or for a new policy that transcends all areas. Do this with the entire staff—including supervisors—present.

The next step is for department managers to come up with a plan to address the obvious needs specific to their area. *Note: The survey should ask the anonymous participants for information like what area they work in and who their supervisor is. This is done so any positive or negative responses can be disclosed to the correct leaders.* With the general manager of the operation in attendance—which serves numerous purposes—managers can next cover each survey question with their department going over both the highs and lows. This should include comments made and the positive and negative percentages. If the supervisors leading the feedback session aren't sure what precipitated a poor response or complaint, ask staff what or where the issue is coming from (as opposed as to whom it's coming from). Even more importantly, the entire group can discuss possible solutions. By using such a tool, a managerial group can monitor morale and correct complications before things get so bad that monumental effort is required to salvage the culture. Remember, if a commitment is made to fix something, it should be handled as quickly as possible followed by publicizing the positive outcome (see: "The Most Important Word").

ESTABLISHING ACCOUNTABILITY

Accountability is a must. In my assignment as an assistant buyer for a department store, I learned straightaway that buyers were held to a rule regarding advertisements. If they signed the ad copy proof (about a week ahead of the promotional event), it attested that everything including product artwork, photos, descriptions, price, and availability dates was accurate. It was also their personal guarantee that the merchandise was already in the stores. If the product wasn't physically received and available for sale, the buyer could lose their job: the first time they got written up and the second time the company let the offender go. There were always underlings—including yours truly—being sent by our managers down to the distribution center because the product wasn't yet delivered. Distribution was in the lower basement levels of a huge downtown anchor store which consumed almost an entire city block. Our mission was to ask warehouse management to expedite our department's merchandise. It had usually just arrived at the dock, and we needed the logistics group to get it through their operation and out to the destination stores in advance of the newspaper advertisement or mailed sales brochure. In effect, we were pleading to save the jobs of our bosses (the supervising buyers) because their advertised items either hadn't been ordered and/or hadn't arrived at the warehouse in enough time. Logistics' supervision was quite desensitized to our pleas since this was a weekly occurrence involving more than a handful of departments. Even while I was feeling caught between a rock (my buyer) and a hard place (the distribution staff), I couldn't argue with the wisdom for establishing this rule.

If there aren't actual consequences appropriate to the misconduct, expected performance level or deadlines will be compromised (see: "Three Types of Workers"). To balance accountability, however, expectations need to be fair and reasonable which includes accounting for extenuating circumstances when they occur (see: "The Blame Game").

Tactfully call out dysfunctional behavior or it will continue. This includes coaching or reprimanding, if appropriate, a member of the staff who misrepresents the facts or fails to carry out an assignment (see: "Seek Respect Before Friendship"). *Warning: Please don't take your frustrations out on the wrong person because you're upset over a performance failure of which you've just become aware.* When I began working at an established firm in the Mountain West, we had a long-term employee get in a fight. When others arrived to break it up, the employee was inside a trailer punching another man. Both employees were suspended while an investigation was conducted. To my surprise, when we pulled the apparent aggressor's HR file, it revealed more than a dozen documented corrective discussions (none of which involved physical confrontations). As recollection serves me, this person had been with the company somewhere between 15 and 20 years. As a young man, he was a prospect to play professional football when a car accident with injury ended that dream. Although he didn't require any physical accommodation to perform his job with us, his athletic prowess had been lessened. After concluding our inquiry, we recommended that the now-confirmed assailant be terminated. However, the man in charge of human resources told my boss we couldn't carry out our intended action, partially because of the employee's earlier misfortune. I privately asked my boss, "If this character came to work with a weapon, would that also be overlooked?"

Soon thereafter, I had a frank conversation with the offender and acknowledged it would be hard to terminate him unless he had another physical outburst, something he had undoubtedly already figured out on his own. On the other hand, I shared my conclusion that it was permissible for me to suspend him without pay for three days anytime he violated less egregious rules. He was diplomatically informed that anytime he clearly stepped over a line, I would at a minimum exercise this option and perhaps more if warranted. That was the last time a suspension was necessary because he didn't want a smaller paycheck. *Note: This approach isn't guaranteed to work on everyone, especially the small portion of the population who don't care about the extra money or the job.*

This same employee was always complaining about his current manager. Over the course of my tenure, he went through three. I'd been at the company for about six years when this disgruntled worker came into my office to complain about his third supervisor. After hearing him out, I expressed that I'd heard this all before and my conclusion was that he was the main source of the problem, particularly since his first two bosses had been very well liked by staff and peers. Furthermore, all three of the managers had the same complaints about him, which were now supported by at least 13 documented discussions in his file. The conversation ended with me conveying I wasn't on a witch hunt (proven by the fact I only responded to valid complaints), but (a) my opinion had been formed after a lot of personal involvement, and (b) my original promise to hold him accountable—including suspension or termination, if necessary—was still in force.

He was rather quiet and I sincerely expressed that I didn't dislike him but that on occasion some of his conduct was quite unacceptable. However, he had proven an ability to avoid stepping out of line for extended periods. My commitment was to be as fair as possible with everyone on the team. After our conversation, I don't recall any problems for the remainder of my tenure. We'd done our best to make him accountable within a less-than-ideal framework. Even though it wasn't anywhere close to perfect, at least the employee felt the need to perform his job satisfactorily, including never assailing or harassing anyone again.

Keep in mind that most individuals need to feel like their performance will be monitored and evaluated (see: "Three Types of Workers"). Don't forget that positive recognition—including reasonable rewards (if you're a budget owner, include them in your financial submission)—should follow when they hit or exceed the mark or exhibit exemplary behaviors. Fair consequences, including coaching, should be imposed when they don't measure up to the standard (see: "Set Higher Standards").

As this relates to scheduling, it's important to be flexible to accommodate the personal needs of our workforce, but it should also be made clear that in certain situations employees should come in early, take a shorter lunch, or stay late if needed to get their work done (see: "Time Off"). Sometimes you'll find that under this expectation, personnel suddenly start managing their time better. If deadlines need to be extended it should be requested in advance, not after deadlines are missed.

When developing targets for an employee's next performance period, involve the employee as appropriate and allocate a percentage of review points to the position description responsibilities in addition to each goal at the beginning of the year. During periodic evaluations, discuss and reinforce the performance expectations so each worker knows where you need them to focus their energy. For instance, "Your four goals and objectives will individually be worth ten points (collectively, 40/100 points on your review); the balance will be associated with your documented responsibilities."

During reviews, after small talk to put you both at ease, your next question might be, "In relation to your responsibilities and goals, what do you believe you're doing well?" Then ask, "Where are you not meeting the challenges?" This will give you a better sense of how your team member sees their contribution (see: "Chip on Our Shoulder?"). If you're trying to bridge the gap between where you see the employee versus their self-perception, this is a good place to begin.

MEET REGULARLY WITH DIRECT REPORTS

My diligence in consistently scheduling staff meetings has been commendable, but I've struggled to hold routine sit-down conversations with my direct reports. I've done it well for extended periods, but at other times I've depended too much on informally communicating concerns and questions. Although I try to seek out and be accessible to my management team, I wish I'd unfailingly incorporated formal one-on-one chats. Maybe when I started to slip, I could have asked my administrative assistant to switch to bi-monthly meetings. When I let my discipline slide, it remained in my mind because I understood the worthwhile nature of the practice.

In preparation for these individual sessions (when I was having them consistently), I customarily shared a standardized agenda, so neither party forgot important subject matter. It had focus areas like expenses, sales, morale, training, capital expenditures and resource needs, hiring plans, service standard performance, and other elements critical to our operation. If you give your direct reports a copy of the list beforehand, conscientious managers will come better prepared to discuss each of the issues. Even if there's nothing to discuss about a bullet point, it's important to know if things are at an acceptable state. It's also revealing if you later discover a staff member had a chance to inform you of a need or challenge but chose not to do so.

This activity is a great time saver for both parties. It helps limit impromptu interruptions to your schedule when a direct report needs advice, input, or to partner with you on something. If you don't meet regularly with your supervisor, they'll start looking for opportunities to meet informally. This often happens at inconvenient times. Even when a supervisor is able to connect with you spur of the moment, sometimes when they leave your office and get down the hall, they'll remember something else and come back to discuss it. Over several days it consumes more time to come into your office on a handful of different occasions than if they utilize just one session to discuss everything. Additionally, it eliminates wasted time when efforts are put on hold while they track you down for approval. Conversely, it empowers them to act on projects discussed and blessed in advance. It's the same principle as hitting every green light while driving down a busy street, or even more applicable, trying to avoid the frequent starts and stops in a production setting which negatively impact productivity. If you don't encourage planned communication, you're not training your team members to be organized; chances are, they're most likely interacting with their peers and subordinates in the same manner.

As a manager, be flexible and able to cope with interruptions. This requires patience and I've had to keep working at it myself. You don't want to disregard important information, so go ahead and hear the report. To limit future interruptions without discouraging people from seeking you out, explain, "I want to spend sufficient time with you to discuss all of your concerns and duties. Please come to our next session prepared to discuss any pertinent issues."

SECTION THREE

MOTIVATION

FAILING TAKES ENERGY

Winners and losers can both expend a lot of energy. Winners focus on evaluating, planning, communicating, executing, following up, and re-evaluating. These activities lead to accomplishment and progress.

Unless they've checked out entirely, losers focus on criticizing, complaining, taking more credit than they earned, keeping information to themselves, undermining or blaming others, excuse making, and generally trying to get ahead without focusing on the most important tasks at hand. None of this activity leads to anything constructive. Perhaps Thomas Edison's words might inspire those who need encouragement: "If we all did all the things we're capable of doing, we would literally astound ourselves."[26]

Winning usually takes more energy, but the payoff is so much greater. Would you rather work at 90% to 100% of your capacity and take pleasure in what you helped achieve, or work at 60% to 70% of your ability and have very little or nothing to show? If you want to decide where you fit in (self-reflection is admittedly very difficult), look at your current or most

---

[26] Quoted in Ford, Martin E. *Motivating Humans: Goals, Emotions, and Personal Agency Beliefs*. Sage Publications, Inc. 1992, p. 17.

recent job and see if you can enumerate what you and your teams attained that was meaningful (see: "Earn More Than We're Paid").

If you're trying to break a unit's cycle of failure, keep in mind that it's hard for people expending 100% effort to field disapproval even if they're not hitting expected targets (see: "Research Reoccurring Problems to the Individual" and "Always Give Our Best"). This is because it's difficult for them to differentiate between effort and effectiveness. They're going to need accomplished leadership to realize this goal. Make it clear that you need their efforts to be focused, performing either old or new tasks in a more effective and efficient manner rather than working more hours if they already have excessive schedules. This may help them adopt a new course of action for expending their energy. Rather than wondering how they can give more, help them focus on how they can contribute better.

ONE TEAM

One day, I suggested to my boss that we should invite one of the extremely difficult divisional managers to lunch so we could try to come to some level of mutual understanding. Over the years this merchandising executive didn't want to have a dialogue regarding resolving ongoing challenges and was extremely quick to blame our division for any problems. My boss, feeling he had already bent over backwards, sarcastically replied, "The only reason I would go to lunch with him would be to feed him eggs." I'm embarrassed to admit I thought his comment was very funny. Of course he didn't mean it, but it demonstrated how communication can break down when one party reacts to another's unwillingness to sincerely engage in problem solving. Teamwork is an essential element of organizational achievement.

During one company's problematic period—which ultimately led to its demise—my assistant and I were sitting in my office one day second-guessing the decisions being made by senior management. Among other things, we were grousing about the loss of the energy manager. The man running the distribution center walked by and listened to some of our conversation. He chimed in with, "I don't believe they think we know enough to help them make better decisions." Sadly, not only was teamwork dissipating throughout the corporation, including among our division, but the company was failing fast. For our part, this kind of discussion had no benefit during difficult times (see: "Take the High Road" and "Failing Takes Energy"). I don't know if it would have been enough to make a difference, but I really wish the company had developed a much greater culture of collaboration. Perhaps if senior management would have tapped into the talented pool of middle managers to address difficulties earlier, the firm could have survived and even thrived. Too often those at the head feel it's a sign of weakness when they don't have all of the solutions.

At all levels of business the norm should be to communicate honestly. Strive to cooperate and join forces with those in and out of your area, focusing on objectives that will help you overcome challenges the venture faces. Help coworkers achieve worthwhile goals. Stop making everything a competition, especially within your own organization. You can make a difference, since people are drawn to you when passion is exhibited about their efforts. In fact, one of the best things you can do to create unity is to occasionally take one for the team, as long as it's not morally objectionable and you have enough affirmative standing (see: "The Most Important Word").

Similarly, whether you oversee a large facility or small department, consider if your staff's tasks are simple enough that team members can cross-train. Establish a rule that when feasible, the shift doesn't go home until everyone's duties are complete. This may not be possible in departments like IT, marketing, accounting, or where everyone's specialty requires significant formal education, training, or experience. But even in these areas, it unites coworkers when everyone pitches in on big projects, like hosting a convention or grand opening, and when staff members can perform general functions or assist in someone else's discipline. In the warehouses and distribution centers in which I've worked, this has been a worthwhile practice when consistently and thoughtfully applied. It's best facilitated by a brief meeting among managers right before or after the start of each day shift. It provides a forum to quickly share department workloads, coordinate interdepartmental movement of team members, and develop short-term contingency plans for resources.

The practice of moving cross-trained employees out of departments with a lighter workload into busier areas helps preserve achievement of service standards, avoid unnecessary overtime, and prevent the use of temporary workforce services (see: "Controlling and Utilizing Overtime"). *A reminder: Temporary employees can be helpful, but they're not as efficient and error-free as your own staff. They require more training and oversight. Since you pay a fee beyond their rate (often near the rate of your new hires) to the agency, units per hour and cost per unit goals can suffer. They do have value in certain scenarios, however.*

Although some employees resist working in a different department, often because they dislike change, it can still become positive for them if the management team is communicative and appreciative. This includes explaining to individuals shifting elsewhere what the workload objectives are and then praising their contributions afterward. Who doesn't enjoy genuine recognition? Furthermore, accuracy and efficiency are fostered when work units are aware of the demands and expectations other work groups face. Teamwork improves because it's usually harder to dislike someone when you've worked with them. As my father would say, "A change is as good as a rest."

Allow me to use a modest experience from my past. When I neared the end of my junior year, our high school basketball coach left and went on to a college job. He later told us he thought it was a good year to leave. We took that to mean that the upcoming senior class, which we helped

CONCEPTS OF MANAGING

comprise, didn't look very promising when compared to his previous teams, two of which played for the state championship.

Five of us were from a small farming community whose students were bused to a larger adjacent town that provided most of the student body. Three of us were seniors, one was a junior, plus a sophomore (a senior's younger brother). We three eldest had played ball together hour upon hour, almost every day since we were freshman. Running the plays and knowing where everyone was on the floor became second nature. Our previous coaches and assistant coaches had drilled into us the philosophy that if a player got open, he got the ball. It was an unspoken understanding that he should take the shot even if he had gone cold shooting. We didn't want his defender collapsing to double team someone else.

Despite some new direction, with our new coach (a man in his first head coaching job) we made a good run in the tournament. The three seniors averaged 10 to 15 points per game scoring but there were more than a few games that season when four and five team members each scored in double figures. It was a balanced group effort. None of us were worried about trying to be stars; although a few individual honors were garnered, we were just trying to win games. Together we were division champs. In the state tournament we faced four schools with student bodies up to four times larger than ours. We lost to the team who ended up claiming the title, but we beat several other talent-laden opponents over the course of the season and tournament. This included the team who had been picked earlier to win it all (their five starters all went on to play ball at NCAA Division I universities). Many of us remain close to this day.

Not exactly *Hoosiers*, but okay for an undersized team that wasn't supposed to accomplish anything of note. It's pretty apparent we were performing very close to our level of competence. From all of the high schools in the state, only four or five seniors probably played on the state championship team that year. That's out of how many students who, (a) wanted to play ball, but didn't make the team, (b) made the team, but didn't get to play much, and (c) played, but didn't win it all. I say this because you need to celebrate your team's accomplishments, even if it's not for a national title or world crown. If you planned carefully, practiced as much as reasonable, and gave your best, then celebrate how well you did.

Note: I thought you might enjoy a little side story. The opposing coach of the team mentioned was known for his temper and antics, like seat-belting himself to the bench to avoid technical fouls. After the game, one of our younger teammates who didn't see much on-court action that year came back from the showers still dry. When asked, "Why didn't you shower?" he said, "I couldn't. Their coach told me to get out of there." Our coach went to investigate and found their head coach, with whom he was acquainted, showering with his suit on. He asked, "Is everything alright?" "Yeah, yeah, everything's okay." Our teammate was sent back to the showers without further incident.

At a much, much higher level were the amazing Boston Celtics. When I was a young child I never pulled for them, but they won an incredible number of championships over a couple of decades. The team was built around rather unglamorous players—in my juvenile opinion—like Bailey Howell, Bill Russell, Sam Jones, Casey Jones, Tommy Heinsohn, Bob Cousy, and John Havlicek. They won eleven championships over twelve years (1957–69) against teams like the LA Lakers which was loaded with superstars like Wilt Chamberlain, Jerry West, and Elgin Baylor. By winning, some of these Boston players became Hall of Famers, but they were immortalized primarily as a result of their success as a team and secondarily upon their individual statistics. They played together for years and developed amazing championship chemistry. Each member of the Celtics was a role player who appreciated how important their contribution was to their combined success. They didn't leave the team to take a bigger contract; they stood together and achieved something extraordinary. Your workplace can benefit from the same approach and coherence. Working as a team, you can accomplish results beyond expectations.

ASK, DON'T COMMAND

Be polite when asking a staff member to perform a task. Saying, "Would you please…," "May I ask a favor?," or "Would you be kind enough to do this for me?" isn't a sign of weakness. Only on a handful of occasions have I experienced the attitude-laced response, "I don't want to do that." If this happens, simply offer, "You don't understand. I'm making a request that falls within the scope of your job and I'm just trying to be pleasant about it. However, I expect you to comply." It doesn't have to be a military command to get an individual to follow directions (see: "Control the Situation"). Ask nicely. When they finish, tell them you appreciate their effort (see: "Genuine Concern and Frequent Appreciation"). In time, they will recognize that this is how you request others to perform assignments. It's a much more pleasant way to conduct business.

Almost always try to say thanks in person whenever practical; granted, there are a few occasions where this might send a mixed message. Sure, most of the tasks accomplished are part of their job description, but we should engage in social pleasantries whenever possible. It's another way we can positively impact workplace culture.

WALKING THE WALK

This is one of my favorite pieces of advice because it was a lesson taught to me by my dad, who spent many years in the construction industry. He stated, "Don't ask someone to do something you wouldn't." It is a principle I saw him live again and again. Consider the danger of cave-ins faced by construction workers digging trenches for projects like large pipelines. Occasionally workers get buried during a cave-in and sometimes tragically can't be rescued fast enough to avoid suffocation. While writing this chapter, a man working on a swimming pool installation in my hometown was killed by a collapsed earthen wall. A friend of mine survived a cave-in and struggled for years to overcome the effects of oxygen deprivation.

Some supervisors oversee dangerous projects standing safely above and outside the trench. When my father was a foreman, he refused to take the cautious approach but rather insisted upon being down in the channel whenever one of his workers was exposed to risk. He wasn't doing the same amount of labor as they were, but he helped whenever needed. He'd done this type of work before, and he was still willing to face the same threat.

The only time I'm aware of him deviating was when they'd finished laying a long pipeline and it need to be inspected for leaks. This required someone to crawl on their hands and knees for a quarter mile through the tube. Like me, my dad was claustrophobic. He called the crew together and told them he needed a volunteer. He admitted it was a job he couldn't perform and offered a fair incentive to anybody who could, but he wouldn't demand it. One man without claustrophobia happily volunteered. Even when my father found it necessary to make an exception to his creed, he was upfront instead of evading the issue.

Historians helped America canonize General George W. Patton. He was a charismatic leader, toting ivory- (not pearl-) handled forty-five pistols strapped to his side, who believed he was born to lead men into battle. Soldiers followed him because he refused the safety of the rear position. He was often on the front lines exposed to danger in the heat of battle, and they willingly followed him into harm's way.

Although we may never be in a similar situation, the advice still pertains. If we find it necessary to ask people to work long hours on a weekend (for inventory or whatever), travel to an unpleasant destination, or perform an undesirable task, we should model the way by either being there or having taken our turn earlier (see: "Paying Your Dues"). It's wrong to ask others to sacrifice in a manner you're not willing to do yourself.

CONCEPTS OF MANAGING

SET HIGHER STANDARDS

This topic relates to a host of goals and objectives encountered in the workplace, including customer satisfaction, deadlines, and profit and loss performance. Allow me to contrast two environments I've encountered. In one, I came upon several receiving department employees sitting down for an extended period when not on break. When I asked their manager what was going on, he said they'd just worked very hard unloading a trailer and needed rest. In the other setting, the receiving manager had a doorbell installed at the loading dock so when it gently chimed over the paging system staff could rush to the receiving area. Their goal was to set and maintain a company-wide record for how quickly they could unload a completely full, incoming 48' trailer of new merchandise (as I recall, their record was less than 35 minutes). They were permitted to turn a stereo up to a volume that wouldn't carry outside the dock area but would provide music to pace their effort. Of course, they didn't work at this tempo all the time, but they stayed busily engaged. Which employees enjoyed their jobs more? I can assure you it was the latter, in some measure because their supervisor focused the team on goals, tried to make work enjoyable, and recognized them personally and with senior management for their achievements. Some had career aspirations, a few made suggestions that were adopted, most were quick to engage in pleasant conversations with leadership, and I don't remember any complainers. I believe this attitude helped advance their careers.

You don't have to live by anyone else's values when they're sub-standard or mediocre. Strive to make certain your department or division has the highest standards and performance in the company. This will bring your staff distinction and further opportunities (see: "The Most Important Word"). A byproduct is gaining more of the available pie regarding compensation, assets, and other considerations for employees.

My first introduction to this was when I was assigned to be an assistant manager for a sizable store. The store manager (my new boss) took me on a tour my first day. My experience to that point included running two medium-sized units, but as we walked the ample back-stock areas I was amazed at how well everything was organized. To illustrate, all of the towels were folded, color-coded, and neatly stacked just as they would be on the sales floor. We met some employees hard at work and my director pointed out that a few of the towels weren't folded correctly and mentioned a few cardboard boxes casually tossed aside. He reminded them to make sure they took care of these oversights before they left for other duties. What a tyrant. Didn't he appreciate how good everything else looked? His expectation caught me off guard, so I tried to tactfully ask if he seriously hoped for near-perfection. He said it was the company standard, but most store managers chose not to enforce it to that degree. He, however, felt it was the right thing to do and that it ultimately saved time in restocking the sales floor. Why fold a towel poorly once and then refold it correctly, when you could fold it right the first time (see: "Influencing Impressions" and "Order Serves Success")?

He added that although his staff didn't always hit the standard, it was highly advisable not to lower it. If they periodically hit the mark for things like a visit from an executive, at least they'd know it was achievable. If they didn't always maintain that level of excellence in presentation, they would frequently touch it. If he lowered the goal, they'd usually operate beneath the standard and find it increasingly difficult to achieve or recover the higher target no matter what the occasion. If he allowed them to compromise or lower requirements, everything would shift downward. Once he had accepted less, it would be very difficult to reinstitute and achieve the greater objective. He also mentioned that while employees might periodically test his resolve, they'd rise to the standard if fostered through consistent communication.

This principle was reinforced when I was promoted to store manager at a different location with that same company. The domestics' department manager had a towel section on the sales floor with no towel out of place.

CONCEPTS OF MANAGING

As soon as a customer left, one of the employees would hurry to the fixtures to refold and replace any un-purchased towels. Prior to my arrival, this attention to detail was given a sustaining boost when the company president came to the store and said the presentation of the towel fixtures was so impeccable, she was sending up a film crew so she could show it to the rest of the company. Even after the original department manager had moved to another assignment, the employees continued to maintain this extraordinary state of merchandise presentation. All new employees were immediately indoctrinated by existing employees. Management didn't need to get involved, although common sense dictated that they continue to recognize the efforts. This was the best towel area in the entire company (almost 200 stores). It had developed a life of its own.

Another illustration involves a very capable maintenance manager with whom I had the privilege of working while we were both employed at a facility with an overly lenient attendance policy. To the best of my recollection, an employee could have up to twenty-one unapproved absences in a rolling calendar year (an entire month of workdays) before they lost their job. His department's staff was small and he needed all of them to be present to get the job done. He had about four journeyman-level technicians, an apprentice, and three or four other helpers and custodians. A couple of his junior staff began mirroring the excessive absences of poor employees in the rest of the facility. As soon as he observed this change, he told each of them, "I don't care if other people in the company can have twenty-one absences per year before they lose their jobs. It's not acceptable conduct in this department. Being ill with a doctor's note [required for approved absences] is understandable and not an issue. We have a very generous personal time-off allowance, so if you have more than a couple of unapproved absences a year, I'll interpret that to mean you lack consideration for the team. I may not be able to terminate you, but I am able to assign you less-desirable tasks until I see an improvement; if it goes unaddressed, it will reflect in your review. You're unfairly burdening the rest of the maintenance team by not showing up." He required dedication from his staff, because when the department was left shorthanded, the remaining group employees had to shoulder the additional workload (see: "Everyone Doing Their Share").

Some people get up and go to work when they don't feel up to it. They must be very sick to call in (though I don't advocate risking health or spreading illness). Others, with less commitment to the job and team, are easily dissuaded from going in for the slightest of reasons. The maintenance manager knew that for his unit to achieve all of their goals and gain the benefits of a top-notch department, he needed to use every driving impetus available. He was unwilling to allow attendance guidelines that cultured mediocrity to negatively influence the standards he had. He expected team members to carry their fair share of the load and to pull themselves up by their bootstraps because other people throughout the operation depended on them to keep the equipment and facility operational.

We've probably all encountered situations where supervisors knew their staff was intentionally working slower or with less effort than they should. An inexperienced supervisor will once in a while bemoan not having engineered standards against which they can compare employee performance. My suggestion under these conditions has become unwavering. Have the supervisor personally carry out the following experiment. Start with any central task suspected of under-performance. Engage in the effort for at least fifty-five minutes (more than fair allowance for 30 minutes of break time spread over the workday), if not for longer. Select a normal content workload and continue at a steady pace that can be sustained all day long. Once they have personal familiarity with the task, a good performance standard can be established. *Note: Of course, this exercise needs to be rolled out by repeating the practice for all basic duties the workers in the area are required to perform on a regular basis.*

Announcing the standard to everyone engaged in this particular function is the litmus test. If over a monthlong period your better employees approach or exceed the target, you know it's fair. If you really want to, you can make a 90% goal the minimum acceptable level. Initially, the standard could be raised or lowered, but unless there has been a process or equipment change only make the adjustment once to avoid allowing it to become a matter of constant negotiation. Perhaps your company won't let you terminate someone who doesn't stay within standard, but it becomes data you can use for reviews, awarding favorable assignments, or even promotions. Of course, your staff will come with exceptions, but now you can use the standard to suggest higher productivity on easier workloads and vice versa. You don't have to lower the goal to account for the worst-case scenario, just offer a reduced target for specific tasks now that you're aware of what can be accomplished with reasonable effort. Since goal setting is proven to be the best motivation method, equitable but also achievable performance levels will now be in place to facilitate the team's efforts to set themselves apart.

GENUINE CONCERN AND FREQUENT APPRECIATION

Work can be trying and difficult, but life is short and as leaders we should try to make it enjoyable, interesting, challenging, and rewarding for those who labor at our side (see: "Maintain Balance"). While observing lines of propriety, take the opportunity to show an interest in team members. This culture fosters open and honest communication, helps individuals feel stronger commitment to achieving goals, and it's the right way to treat people.

From junior high into high school and then through the first four years of college, I was never too far from my best friend. We played a lot of basketball together (even though he had no idea what an "assist" was), dated some of the same young women (not at the same time), worked together for several years at a bank, studied together occasionally, and had more fun than we deserved. Our bond strengthened even more as he stood by me during a difficult period in my mid-twenties. I got married, moved away, moved back, moved away again, and finally ended up living across the street from him in my late forties. Even though we stayed in touch over the years and saw each other when my wife and I visited family, life changed us both. The change in him that stood out the most was how he became so supportive and complimentary, especially since I joked that he never said anything nice to me the first dozen years of our friendship. His wonderful wife certainly had much to do with this improvement. Now almost every time I see him, he's quick to say kind and insightful things about my children, my wife, and me. He freely shares his admiration of what we've accomplished and how we conduct ourselves. I'm trying to incorporate that characteristic, but I'm way behind his progress.

My friend also passes the litmus test for authenticity. Most of my life I've been hypersensitive to insincerity. If my buddy was being phony, I would have known it the moment it slipped out of his mouth. In our youth, we were awfully sarcastic, and I was just waiting to catch him shelling out dual meanings. Perhaps I can best illustrate this by stating how much I cringe anytime an acquaintance uses the term "special" to describe someone. To me, using this word falls somewhere between laziness and disingenuousness. If they say, "Oh, they're such a special person," I feel they should at least care enough to clarify, "They're very encouraging," "They're very creative," or anything else more specific.

Learn from the insensitivity of my early years and commit to sincerely saying thank you as often as possible whenever merited. When you express appreciation, take time to elaborate why you're grateful and do so with genuine feeling. I recall an experience where I was given an assignment by the bishop of our congregation (somewhat equivalent to a minister or pastor in a Protestant church) to focus on financial records. There had been some sloppiness previously and it took extra effort over the next six months to correct the monthly bank statement reconciliations from the previous year. The bishop saw me at the church house and realized I was spending extra time in the assignment. He generally knew what I was doing, but not specifically. Nonetheless, he went out of his way every time he saw me at work to convey how appreciative he was for my conscientious effort. His gratitude made me ensure that I finished a rather mundane project while feeling good about completing it.

There was a man I worked with in church youth programs whom both of my sons idolize. Likewise, I consider him a remarkable example and friend. He elicited this kind of respect despite being smaller than average in stature and a little introverted. He wasn't particularly athletic, wealthy, nor remarkably charismatic. Nevertheless, the quality that drew my sons to him and made me forever grateful for our association was his selfless interest in the youth. He always brought extra gear like gloves and sleeping bags to campouts or activities in case the boys—including his own sons—forgot essential items. He frequently asked how they were doing in school or inquired about their other interests. He then listened as they talked (another way to show concern and appreciation). It was from him that I learned the people we care about aren't the ones who try to impress everybody, but rather the ones who care about others. Most down-to-earth people don't want to be around someone who's self-centered even if they drive an expensive car, brag about association with celebrities, or happen to be a scratch golfer. Why else are parents—especially mothers and grandparents—so beloved by future generations, even if they've gone out of style in their interests, dress, or technical skills? An aphorism from generations preceding mine offered, "People don't come to your home to see the furniture; they come to see you." A line frequently attributed to Theodore Roosevelt wisely states it another way: "Nobody cares how much you know until they know how much you care."[27]

I repeat, be enthusiastically grateful whenever you remember to do so.

---

[27] Quoted in "Theodore Roosevelt." *U.S. Office of Personnel Management.* opm.gov/about-us/our-mission-role-history/theodore-roosevelt/. Accessed 11 April 2023.

This helps to compensate for all of the times that we forgot or fail to notice someone else's contributions. This is often the case in a work environment since most supervisors don't work side-by-side with their team throughout the day. Thus, we only occasionally get snapshots of how each staff member performs.

Encourage employees to point out to the boss when one of their peers goes the extra mile. If you're the person in charge, welcome these reports and meaningfully follow up with the contributor. If someone deserves recognition, team members shouldn't wait for management to notice. Tell coworkers what a good job they're doing, and even better, mention it to the supervisor so they can receive added reinforcement. If done correctly, this enriches work environments by providing opportunities to recognize deserving peers. Every member of a team can positively affect morale.

THREE TYPES OF WORKERS

Thinking through the various workforces I've been around, some employees are self-motivated, some are totally unmotivated, and some fall in the middle. Generalizing, maybe 30% to 40% of hourly staff would still work at or near capacity (a steady, but not arduous, pace that can be sustained all day) for forty hours a week if left unsupervised. *Note: This is likely higher in professional work environments comprised of employees with post-high school educations who value autonomy to complete their workload.* Perhaps 10% to 20% of employees might stop working as soon as they realize no one is monitoring them. I've observed this phenomenon on numerous occasions, coming across personnel lounging while not on break to warehouse staff sitting down on the job after their supervisor walks away. Then there are the remaining coworkers who fall in the middle who seem to work around three-fourths of their capacity, less than they would if they were better motivated, and who make up the largest workforce category in most environments. Ostensively, these employees will observe the other two groups and decide which has the better deal or has made the best decision. If no one is rewarded for extra effort or even full effort, team members gravitate towards the behavior of those who do as little as possible. They may not sit down, but they'll certainly slow down. On the other hand, if you have achievable and fair incentives in place to reward them, those who fall in the middle are more likely to increase effort to protect their job, and if possible, try to make additional money (see: "Set Higher Standards").

There's a natural tendency for a small percentage of the population to disparage those who work faster or more conscientiously since it reflects poorly on their own contribution (see: "Earn More Than We're Paid"). People recognized as top performers can have others tell them, "You've got to slow down. You're making us look bad."

To illustrate, early in his career one of my brothers worked in the finance division for a major U.S. automaker. He received a company vehicle to be used only for business travel. Because he didn't use the car for personal use, several of his coworkers confronted him: "You're causing a real problem. We're all reporting twenty-five hundred miles a month for work-related mileage and you're only detailing fifteen hundred."

This phenomenon is also illustrated by the crab mentality metaphor: if you place crabs in a pot, you can take the lid off and none of them will be able to make their escape. When one crab tries to crawl out, others reach up and pull it back in.[28] As a leader, you need to counter these tendencies early on by helping the entire department see how top performers help the team achieve their target goals (the positive approach). Then, if necessary, communicate on an individual basis that you won't tolerate any harassment (the negative approach when necessary).

To merit my assertion, let me share some thoughts about Urban Meyer, a college football coach who won three national championships: "Meyer

---

[28] Miller, Carliss. D. "A Phenomenological Analysis of the Crabs in the Barrel Syndrome." *Academy of Management Annual Meeting Proceedings*, vol. 2015, no. 1, Jan. 2015, p. 1. *EBSCOhost*, doi.org/10.5465/AMBPP.2015.13710abstract.

read that [John] Wooden had a hard time early in his career favoring players, something Meyer could relate to. 'There's certain players that I love and there's other ones I can't stand,' he said. 'If you're saying that's not true, you're not being honest. I love the guys who go to class, I love the guys who live right and I love the guys who are great football players.'"[29] Further, "The Florida coaches even make academics competitive, breaking down the players into three categories: scarlet, red and gold. The scarlet players are considered high risk and have all their classes checked. The red players are watched closely. The gold players don't have any classes checked and aren't required to attend study tables."[30] In other words, reward extra effort.

WHAT ABOUT YOUR MOTIVATION?

What motivates you? Is it a reward you're seeking, another person's love, or fear of a consequence? At different times, each of these factors has moved me into action. A variation of this concept was developed by psychologist David C. McClelland and is known as Human Motivation Need Theory. My first exposure to this was in the context of why some personalities chose certain careers and what made up their strongest desires. To some degree, we're all influenced by the following:

- <u>Power Motive</u>: Individuals that relish competition, like controlling or influencing others, and enjoy the associated status of their positions.

---

[29] Thamel, Pete. "Meyer Uses Behavior Modification for Florida Players. *NYTimes*. 24 July 2005. nytimes.com/2005/07/24/sports/ncaafootball/meyer-uses-behavior-modification-for-florida-players.html?searchResultPosition=1. Accessed 11 April 2023.
[30] Thamel, Pete. "Meyer Uses Behavior Modification for Florida Players. *NYTimes*. 24 July 2005. nytimes.com/2005/07/24/sports/ncaafootball/meyer-uses-behavior-modification-for-florida-players.html?searchResultPosition=1. Accessed 11 April 2023.

- <u>Affiliation Motive</u>: People who value relationships, such as group interaction, and appreciate collaboration.
- <u>Achievement Motive</u>: Those who like to achieve goals, often enjoy working alone, and welcome feedback.[31]

All three motives should be accompanied by some advice. In my opinion, it's better to incorporate each of these qualities into our life rather than only one. Even though one drive may dominate, we're better served by not totally suppressing the other two. What are power and achievement if there's no one with whom to share? What is affiliation if we're not achieving good for others? From this perspective, it's advisable to commend others but not seek their applause in return. Seeking acclaim from others—especially without earning it—is a perilous opiate. This path results in shifting attention to obtaining praise rather than engaging in the acts that merit it (see: "Give the Credit to the Team"). Furthermore, it's better to have someone else extol your accomplishments rather than to tirelessly promote yourself. Don't spend time boasting. Limit efforts to only accurately publicize what is necessary to recognize the team, to secure needed resources and opportunities, or to diplomatically respond to inaccurate depictions of performance.

A quote misattributed to Winston Churchill but inspiring nonetheless states, "We make a living by what we get, we make a life by what we give."[32] Seek satisfaction through helping others develop and be content with the natural byproducts of your effort. There's no lack of people who need to be listened to, encouraged, and reinforced. Help them with their honorable aspirations. It's noble to be a catalyst and assist everyday people in accomplishing things they think are beyond their reach. Find fulfillment in seeing what people can become and watching them achieve.

---

[31] McClelland, David C. *Human Motivation*. U of Cambridge, 1987. McClelland also addresses the avoidance motive.

[32] "Winston Churchill: Misattributed." *WikiQuote*. 6 April 2023. en.wikiquote.org/wiki/Winston_Churchill. Accessed 11 April 2023.

This improves their life and the lives of those with whom they come in contact. Last but not least, learn to care for those with whom you disagree or don't share interests. I strive to engrain these traits more firmly in my own character.

As you set out on this quest, don't try to do it alone. Associate with good people who have admirable aspirations. When possible, learn from the talented people you encounter, but remember their fallibility and don't be undiscerning when you stumble upon their weaknesses (see: "Find a Mentor"). Adopt the positive but don't mimic the undesirable. Be very cautious and, if necessary, maintain a safe distance from people who are grossly negative or clearly users, takers, or abusers.

Much of our success comes as a positive consequence of developing good habits. A disputed Michelangelo statement declares, "If people knew how hard I had to work to gain my mastery, it would not seem so wonderful at all."[33] I confess this book would have been written years sooner if I had the discipline to write every day. Recognize that good habits are hard to start and continue—it takes effort. Consider the example of learning to play a musical instrument and the consistent practice required. That being said, don't quit trying if you don't hit the daily targets of perfection you've created in your mind. Like a New Year's resolution, judge success by how many times you honored or performed the resolution and not by how many times you failed. If you planned to exercise five days a week and only average three, you've still succeeded in improving your activity.

On the other hand, the difference with bad habits is that they're much, much easier to begin and much, much harder to stop. Overindulging in anything is almost guaranteed to be injurious, whether it's unhealthy food, laziness, or recreational drugs.

You become what you spend your time contemplating. When you get up in the morning, what are you thinking about? Are you mulling how

---

[33] "Michelangelo: Disputed." *WikiQuote*. 26 February 2023. en.wikiquote.org/wiki/Michelangelo. Accessed 11 April 2023.

to assist family, friends, and humanity, or are you considering swindling someone out of money or credit for an accomplishment you have no right to claim?

Abraham Maslow taught about the various levels of self-actualization.[34] We begin by taking care of life's necessities, but individuals who advance beyond this sooner—self-actualizing people—are those who strive to achieve good and noble things. These are the people who make a difference.

My family has benefited from such acts of goodness and kindness. One of my spouse's high school classmates stands out. She called my wife almost every Sunday morning for years while we lived thousands of miles away, because she knew she was staying home with our chronically ill daughter. I took the other children to church (these were the roles we agreed upon) and so it was a time when my dear companion undoubtedly felt left out and needed a friend to ease the burden. Another experience involved a buddy of mine who dressed himself up as Santa and his Rottweiler as Rudolph to make a Christmas Eve visit to our homebound daughter as she waited for an organ transplant. Then there's also the kindhearted woman who has written weekly note of encouragement to my dear mate, for longer than I can remember, because she sympathizes with her health challenges. The list goes on.

Most of my personal heroes aren't celebrities. Rather, they're individuals I've encountered in life's journey who became great to me by performing acts of kindness: "And out of small things proceedeth that which is great."[35] It's been said that you can change the world one person at a time. The most effective self-improvement plan is losing ourselves in the effort to help others, including our family and friends. Let that be our motivation.

---

[34] Maslow, Abraham H. "A Theory of Human Motivation." *Psychological Review*, vol. 50, no. 4, 1943, pp. 370-396.
[35] *The Doctrine and Covenants of The Church of Jesus Christ of Latter-day Saints*. The Church of Jesus Christ of Latter-day Saints, 1981. Section 64, verse 33.

SECTION FOUR

RELATIONSHIPS

THE BLAME GAME

One of my bosses advocated, "Fix the problem, not the blame." When we focus on the problem, a culture of continuous improvement ensues. If we focus too much on the blame, we create an atmosphere filled with counterproductive behaviors including time-consuming inquisitions, misrepresenting the facts, placing fault on others, or trying to claim innocence. This cycle can perpetuate itself, sometimes for years, if you don't address the paradigm.

No one is perfect, so we need a healthy dose of forgiveness and tolerance. Strike a fine balance between vigilant focus on the corporate mission and becoming mired in recrimination. This isn't to suggest we should permit the same mistake to be made repeatedly while expecting a different result, typified as insanity (see: "Establishing Accountability" and "Micromanage Non-Performers").

Illustrative of this predicament was an episode from several decades ago where my work team had a product that needed to be developed over a six-month period. After repeated delays, our manufacturing and operation teams received the formula just two weeks before launch. There was a mad rush to source a few unusual raw materials. Next was delivery to the third-party manufacturer, whom we'd pleaded with to reserve us a spot in their busy production schedule. The item was manufactured and trucked back to the warehouse to wait for testing, which usually required anywhere from several days up to a week. Finally, we transported the items to the location of the introductory announcement. When the product arrived a day later than promised by product development (not us), they blamed operations for their incompetency when in fact we'd worked a small miracle.

Later on, a senior manager over the labeling department chose to investigate these occurrences and held a limited post-mortem review. Her honorable objective was to get to the bottom of the cycle of inefficiency and finger-pointing. With all concerned parties in attendance, it soon became clear that the departments tasked with formula development and packaging were guilty. Other departments demonstrated through email records that they had the "baton" for less than two weeks of the six-month period allowed, counting several brief touches along the way. Our operations division reveled in the outcome—we were vindicated. The problem was that the blame game ultimately didn't help anything. The manager behind the investigation was now disliked by the offenders because their inefficiencies had been exposed. Their subsequent comments revealed they'd never accepted any guilt. The process never improved because rather than building a bridge to collaboration, it had been burnt down. I'd gotten it wrong thinking it was a great day. It wasn't.

It some ways, this parallels my experience with sensitivity training (also referred to as T-Groups) in graduate school. Our class of about 15 students was sequestered in a large classroom on a Saturday, with two prominent professors serving as observers and facilitators. We engaged in role-playing exercises of somewhat intense situations where our weaknesses (dominating conversations, making up or ignoring the facts, brooding, etc.) would be noticed, and called out, and followed by a pseudo-intervention from the other group members. One of the major drawbacks was that we spent over ten hours critiquing one another and less than two hours trying to build up classmates with damaged egos. In my opinion, a few offensive personalities were spared because they behaved cautiously or disingenuously throughout the session. My takeaway was that the flurry of criticism and blame never brought the group together. Those targeted resented the self-appointed critics. No one wants to work in a group where every minor misstep is immediately run up the flagpole.

Certainly, we need to address and evaluate the source of problems, but like King Solomon we need to apply real wisdom in deciding what mistakes require: (a) little or no coaching because the mistake was unavoidable or parties involved acknowledged the error; or (b) performance improvement coaching because it's occurred too often or is the result of gross neglect.

THE POWER OF RELATIONSHIPS

Maintain contact with individuals you've grown to respect while associating with them. Currently, so many tools like LinkedIn, Twitter, and Facebook make this endeavor easier. At least seven jobs I've held were secured because someone I knew either recommended me or wanted to work with me again.

First, I secured a position as a counselor (connecting with plantation management and directing non-work activities) for an employment agency hiring teenagers to pick pineapple in Hawaii. This was primarily due to my high school basketball coach recommending me to the founder, a close friend of his, with whom he'd also worked.

Second, the man with whom I'd overseen a seasonal workforce in Hawaii got me hired as a salesperson in a department store while I returned to finish college. This employment opportunity culminated in my role as buyer/department manager for the men's area.

Third, while continuing my education I moved from that department store to another after just one phone call. I'd interviewed the owner for a college paper and a classmate was one of his buyers/department managers, whom I replaced when he accepted other employment.

Fourth, the man who hired me out of graduate school offered me a position as one of his store managers when he accepted the role as president of a retail chain on the West Coast. After a few years in this role, a promotion to the director of store services resulted.

Fifth, a former peer offered me a position as a director of distribution. He'd become a VP with a different firm and needed to fill that responsibility.

Sixth, a previous boss offered me a role overseeing logistics at a regional retail chain. I'd also previously worked with several other individuals who made up the senior leadership team.

Seventh, a neighbor and member of our church congregation made me aware of what became my most recent job. I'd also been in the company owner's home several times.

On the other side of the coin, I've offered a fair number of jobs to individuals with whom I'd had earlier association. At the time of writing, four members of my professional staff worked with me at previous businesses. If you're looking for a good worker to fill an open position, it's much more effective to network with former coworkers whom you respect. Why would you prefer to hire someone you've only spent a few hours interviewing and examining, when you know capable, proven candidates personally?

If you're seeking a new position with the help of a former colleague, remember it's a two-way street. They won't help you to secure employment unless they're confident you can navigate a challenging work environment, thus reflecting well on them. The adage, "It's not what you know, it's who you know," should be changed to, "It's who knows what you know."

Be mindful that it's seldom for middle or senior managers to be placed in new positions where it's all smooth sailing. A former boss told me, "They won't hire you unless they need you." Nearly every place where I've worked, there have been significant obstacles to surmount. Somebody had quit, been fired, or a new position had been created because large problems and challenges hadn't been successfully addressed. One new position was in a stereo department that had 20% shortages, when a shortage factor over one or two percent was unacceptable. Another role was running a warehouse on the edge of its capacity and needing a new warehouse management software system, along with a new material handling system. Then there was the offer to work at a retailer where they couldn't logistically keep up with the growth. If you haven't experienced these phenomena yet, you will in the future.

Caution: There have also been people I've known outside of work environments to whom I've offered jobs. This is risky because you haven't observed them in a professional setting. You get to know a lot about someone's skills and potential in a job, but in non-work situations you don't necessarily observe work-related abilities or behaviors. You want team members who can get a job done well and on time, without bringing extra baggage.

LOVE THE ONE WE'RE WITH

A managerial candidate once accepted the position I'd offered him and then a couple of days later subsequently declined in order to accept another job. Not anticipating this complication, when the two other finalists had inquired about the status, I'd told them it was filled. I then found it necessary to reach out to my second choice to extend an offer, after explaining the inopportune sequence of events. After a few months on the job, the new manager shared my supposed faux pas with my boss. They laugh at my expense and I wished it would have transpired differently, especially since it got this unflattering spin. Although a minor incident, it made me aware that this employee didn't always have my back.

Do we really needed to be reminded that we should be loyal to whoever hired us or is putting a payroll check in our hand? The expression, "Don't bite the hand that feeds you," obviously came from experience working on a farm and feeding animals. Who wants a horse that intentionally bites them when offering it an apple?

On one occasion, I hired a man to demolish my old deck and build a larger one. It kept extending into a longer and longer process as the contractor juggled this with other jobs (unusual, right?). Three or four days into the project, the owner and assistant of a yard maintenance company showed up to mow and trim the lawn. When they got close to the site of where the old deck had been, there were building materials lying around the yard not adjacent to, but far outside of, the intended new footprint. The builder told them not to worry about it. Why did he feel he had the right to give my lawn care service direction which would result in killing a sizeable portion of the lawn, starved for sunshine and water before he finally wrapped things up?

When I got home from work, I finished mowing the lawn myself and moved the materials to a more suitable staging area. Add to the equation that I hadn't haggled with either company about their fees and I was a little annoyed. Both service providers fell short of expectation to assume responsible and customer-oriented viewpoints during their exchange. *Note: You can read about transactional analysis in Thomas A. Harris's book* I'm OK—You're OK.[36]

The contractor should have been more sensitive to preserving my yard in light of our arrangement and how much he was being paid. Correspondingly, if the landscape service would have had the pluck to tell the contractor that he already had his instructions, I would have been very favorably impressed. Besides, we already had a gentleman's agreement so he could bill me for any extra work he felt was merited. He could have offered to move the lumber temporarily elsewhere and then return it after mowing. If he encountered resistance, he had my number and could have easily called or texted, allowing me to intervene. While this is a very simple example, I chose it because it shows both parties failing to look out for their customer's best interest. I'm glad this didn't happen on a much larger scale involving a contractual engagement in a business setting.

To facilitate this code of conduct, partner with your supervisor since

---

[36] Harris, Thomas A. *I'm OK—You're OK.* Harper & Row, 1967.

they can protect you if you allow them. Keep them informed of your whereabouts during normal work hours if you're going to be somewhere outside of the office. Remember what is required of you so your boss doesn't have to remember those tasks as well (see: "Was it the Assignment Given?"). Give them updates, especially if you have numerous projects. Lastly, show them real allegiance in both conversation and conduct.

EMPLOYMENT IS A TWO-WAY STREET

Most people are acutely aware of whether or not their employer meets their personal expectations. Very few subordinates examine this relationship from their bosses' perspective, factoring their own performance into the equation. As staff members, do we fulfill our supervisor's needs and, if not, does this justifiably impact how we're regarded? The goal is for both parties to feel positive about the realities of what transpires at work.

Consider the individuals to whom we report and ask, "What do they require from me? Am I keeping them informed? Do I work well with coworkers? Do I carefully analyze the facts before making recommendations? Do I work hard and fast without making avoidable mistakes? When I foresee a large blunder, do I warn my supervisor repeatedly and firmly, but not insubordinately?" Case in point, I used to ask one boss if he wanted me to quit bringing up unaddressed topics I deemed important. He said, "No, bring it up occasionally, so I don't forget it." Another good introspective question is, "Am I positive and loyal?" (see: "What Potential Employers Seek" and "Love the One We're With").

Judge your supervisor's actions from a corporate perspective rather than an individual viewpoint. Recognize that they're trying to make the team succeed. A sports analogy: If you're not starting for the team, does that mean your coach [boss] is a jerk? It might be because you're not accomplishing everything they need from your position, you need to work harder, or you're required in a different role. Perhaps, the coach needs you to bring some energy off the bench when the starters have bogged down. If the game is close, are you on the floor at the end? Why or why not?

At one point in time, a member of my managerial staff became quite critical of my no-nonsense approach when I sensed we needed to ramp up our efforts to handle an impending crisis. Less than a year later, I found it fascinating to see how she reacted to an employee complaining about how insensitive and demanding she had been. Apparently, she never connected the dots and realized she'd been critical of me for similar conduct she subsequently exhibited.

One of the most pertinent questions to ask is, "Do I remember and complete assignments?" (see: "Was it the Assignment Given?"). It isn't your manager's duty to keep reminding you of delegated tasks. People who forget things are frustrating, especially if they require going back and telling them to take care of something they should have already finished. It's difficult enough for a boss to remember everything they need to take care of without recalling all the items their staff should follow up on, though they try.

In the classroom, I tried an exercise where I asked students what qualities they'd like their employer to possess. Then, I've asked them to try and identify the skills and personality traits they think their boss is looking for in an employee (see: "What Potential Employers Seek"). The purpose for this activity is grounded in the belief that most students haven't viewed their relationship with management from the other perspective, just from their own. Many individuals are hypercritical of the people to whom they report and show little empathy for professional or personal circumstances. They expect to be very well taken care of, even when they're not meeting expectations. It's much easier to ask for some consideration of your needs if you're delivering what is expected (see: "The Most Important Word").

No one is perfect, so don't abandon the relationship with your supervisor because of an oversight. There are many divorces in the United States: some 50% of marriages now end in divorce, which means that less than half of people who get married stay married. Can you imagine the rate increase if the first time someone's spouse made a mistake it was grounds for separation? Give your leader a few free passes when they forget to say thanks or whatever else may annoy you. Likewise, don't expect someone else to manage your career for you (see: "Willing to Forgive")—they're busy taking care of their own life.

SMILE AND BE APPROACHABLE

For those of us who aren't charismatic, first impressions are important. Good initial interactions break down barriers and save time by not having to later deal with the unfavorable feelings formed by others. Relationships take enough energy to manage without adding unnecessary obstacles like being perceived as sour or contrary. The more people that value their association with you, the better off you'll be. Friends and business associates can then defend your honor, make you aware of useful information, help you accomplish goals, and much more. If you come across as uncaring, uninterested, or unapproachable you make it difficult for anyone to care about getting to know you.

To start, smile and make eye contact for heaven's sake. It makes a world of difference and is a wonderful aid in facilitating human connection. Feel compelled to earnestly communicate your sincere interest. Dale Carnegie is credited with writing, "If you want to be enthusiastic, act enthusiastic."[37] Try it and discover that emitting warmth and genuine happiness has a noticeable impact.

I almost lost my first job opportunity out of grad school because I wasn't outgoing or warmhearted enough in some social settings. While interviewing with the vice president of a department store chain, I tried to be pleasant and respectful right from the beginning. However, his

---

[37] "Dale Carnegie: Quotes." *Goodreads*. 2023. goodreads.com/quotes/524083-if-you-want-to-be-enthusiastic-act-enthusiastic. Accessed 11 April 2023.

first questions were closed questions like, "Where did you get your undergraduate degree?" or "Are you willing to relocate?" I gave specific and measured responses, without a lot of support detail. He then started asking open-ended questions and I took the opportunity to talk a bit more without rambling. Out of nowhere, he stopped the interview and basically said in only a slightly more tactful way, "Is there something wrong with you? It's like I'm interviewing two different people." After he clarified, I tried to explain that I didn't take his first few questions as an invitation to respond in length and gratefully we finished the interview. He later extended an offer, which I accepted. It was then that I realized I needed to meet people more than halfway. When engaging with others—especially with strangers—I needed to connect in a friendly and approachable manner as rapidly as feasible to put them at ease.

Don't wait for someone else to break the ice. If you don't believe this, the next time you're in a social situation with unfamiliar people like a reception at a business conference, make it a point to smile and engage others in conversation. The basics aren't very complex: (a) introduce yourself briefly, without attempting to impress with job titles or accomplishments; (b) ask open-ended questions which aren't too personal but show interest: "What company are you with?," "What's your role there?," "Have you attended this conference before?," or "Are you presenting?"; (c) avoid the temptation to turn the conversation back to yourself whenever something makes you think of an experience or anecdote;[38] and finally, (d) listen to their answers so you can continue to ask thoughtful questions. If they make inquiries about you, keep the responses brief and return the attention back to them as quickly as possible. If you find this difficult to do and notice that you're talking about yourself a lot, you may have encountered an accomplished conversationalist. Enjoy the moment and try to learn from them.

---

[38] Sociologist Charles Derber calls this behavior "conversational narcissism." For more information, see Chapter 2 in his book, *The Pursuit of Attention: Power and Ego in Everyday Life* (Oxford, 2000).

CONCEPTS OF MANAGING

OUR OWN WORST ENEMY

We need people to view us as a team member who makes significant contributions to the goals of the enterprise. As a rule, be pleasant to work with. If someone asks you for a favor and you decide to do it, you don't gain goodwill if you do it begrudgingly. You'll expend energy carrying it out, but they won't feel indebted to you or appreciative if you act put upon. This also applies to personal relationships. If you go to the movie that your spouse would rather see but complain and hold it over their head, no points are earned when it's our turn to pick.

Be aware that sometimes one character flaw can be so noticeable that it colors all of the positive things we do. It's critical to be aware of our own behavioral disorders, monitor them, and keep them in check. This reminds me of an experience I had working with one such manager when I was living not far from the Great Lakes. At one point in time, he was over manufacturing division's shipping area. He did very well, trained his staff, and hit deadlines. This was one of our more important operational departments and his position was a good springboard to the next management level. However, his obvious flaw was that he had an unhappy disposition and often couldn't work well with some of his peers. Other managers were hesitant to inform him of problems (outbound transportation was involved downstream from other areas). Of course, he made minor mistakes occasionally just like everyone else, but he couldn't help but make a considerable fuss if anyone else had a slip-up. This included situations when the problem was unavoidable: he often complained or made a huge fuss about any extra effort required by his staff. For example, this once comprised going on record about how inconvenient and costly it was for his department to stay late 30 minutes to make sure a rush shipment was loaded on that day's trailers for dispatch. His point was valid, but his communication methods were poor at best and unfortunately directed at other managers who couldn't prevent the situation. Everyone sensed he would bring an issue up again, even weeks later. On the other hand, when he needed to ask others to help they were unwilling because he'd previously confronted them over relatively insignificant oversights or unavoidable circumstances.

This manager demonstrated most of the skills he needed to be promoted, but his superiors didn't want to keep mediating or apologizing for him if he moved up. The only thing that kept him from getting ahead—at least at this company—was that he needed to be more accommodating and to get along with people. Maybe he was afraid he would lose control of his self-perceived tight ship if he didn't make a minor spectacle every time he was a little put out. The rest of us knew being team-oriented wouldn't turn him into the doormat he was worried he'd become. His need for process was so strongly ingrained in his nature that he'd never let that happen. He still would have gotten the job done and undoubtedly would have benefited from reading *How to Win Friends and Influence People* and applying a good dose of Dale Carnegie's approach.[39]

Extend an olive branch to those with whom you don't see eye-to-eye. This also goes for accepting new team members on board. If someone you're close to quits or even is fired, you might cop an attitude with their replacement. If the shoe was on the other foot, how would you feel about joining a company and getting the cold shoulder? I remember several occasions where this happened to me. In one case, after introducing myself to a manager on my team he said something to the effect of, "Well, we'll see if you last any longer than the others." This wasn't a good starting point. I also remember a vice president who didn't try very hard to support or cooperate with new members of the executive leadership group. If you've ever read the book *Iacocca*, you might guess it wasn't long until he was dismissed just like when Lee Iacocca terminated most of his vice presidents after becoming CEO of Ford Motor Company.[40]

At another venture, a new sales and marketing director was hired. To

---

[39] Carnegie, Dale. *How to Win Friends and Influence People*. Simon & Schuster, 1936.
[40] Iacocca, Lee. *Iacocca: An Autobiography*. Bantam, 1984.

establish herself, she made it clear in a senior management meeting that I would be held accountable if my division dropped the ball getting any new products out or if we ran out of stock. Some of this came from discussions with her direct reports, who were quick to blame past failures on other departments. Initially, I made a mistake of reacting to these unsubstantiated claims by stating I would welcome being just held accountable for my job instead of being blamed for things out of our control. I then wised up and recognized my best tactic was to prove that the assertions she'd heard were incorrect. Even though we always tried to operate on a timely basis, we went out of our way to show how responsive we could be. It wouldn't matter if it was a request for information or if it involved remodeling the office she occupied: we would meet or exceed any promises or deadlines. Additionally, I made it a point to greet her kindly, take her side when her position was right, and to stop by occasionally and ask how things were going. This worked very well. We got along decently, and I never heard any further accusations.

The Ancient Greek maxim translated as "Know thyself" was inscribed in the Temple of Apollo at Delphi.[41] Most of us have blind spots about our own performance and need frequent reality checks, as well as internal acknowledge that there may be things we can improve. Examples could include sour dispositions, bending the facts in our favor, withholding damaging information, being late to work, or not fulfilling assignments on time. Being aware of blind spots also means guarding against developing additional bad habits. While attending college, I started working at a department store as an assistant. My boss frequently received phone calls from customers wondering why a special order hadn't arrived or why installation hadn't been scheduled. I overheard him tell customers he'd follow up on an order's status with the vendor when I knew he'd forgotten

---

[41] Plato. *The Dialogues of Plato: Charmides*. Translated by B. Jowett. *Project Gutenberg*. 16 January 2013. gutenberg.org/cache/epub/1580/pg1580-images.html. Accessed 11 April 2023.

to order it altogether. After he took a different job and I was promoted to his role, I continued fielding customer service complaints for his mistakes for several months. I don't know if he understood how his lack of follow-up created extra work for him and frustration for his clients.

If you've been around long enough, you've seen coworkers become lame ducks because they didn't like their job, were mad at their boss, or had recently given notice. They quit giving a full day's effort. On occasion, they try to justify this behavior by listing others who give less-than-full effort. Once you start justifying poor performance, when do you stop? When your dream job does come along, will you be too quick to throw in the towel or blame others at the first sign of adversity? You'll have developed bad habits that will hold both you and your company back.

SEEK RESPECT BEFORE FRIENDSHIP

In writing this book, I've tried not to call upon other management books you may have read, but I've made a few exceptions when concepts are important. In *The 7 Habits of Highly Effective People*, Stephen Covey (unfortunately on sabbatical from my grad school staff while he finished his Ph.D.) wrote that relationships are like bank accounts: you must have more deposits than withdrawals.[42] Second, he counseled, "seek first to understand, then to be understood."[43] This is excellent advice as it prepares you for conciliatory encounters, a vital element in developing healthy workplace relationships. Moreover, be sure to always perform your job to the best of your ability and strive to foster teamwork (see: "Always Give Our Best"). Then, if you invest the effort to sit down with someone with

---

[42] Covey, Stephen R. *The 7 Habits of Highly Effective People: Powerful Lessons in Personal Change.* Free Press, 1989. p. 220.

[43] Covey, Stephen R. *The 7 Habits of Highly Effective People: Powerful Lessons in Personal Change.* Free Press, 1989. p. 235.

whom you're not seeing eye-to-eye and hear them out, they're much more inclined to consider your viewpoint.

Another element of cultivating respect is to realize that people assume how we act in front of them—especially gossiping or backbiting—is how we act when they're not present. If we talk unkindly about someone else in their presence, when they see us laughing with others they might assume we're doing so at their expense (see: "Spend Goodwill, but Carefully").

Friendship is often a natural byproduct of respect. At most of the places where I've worked, the relationships formed continued beyond that job. One successful and engaging manager is a friend with whom I still stay in touch. She gave me permission to tell my version of the following story wherein we didn't see eye to eye. It's relevant because afterward we sat down and talked our feelings through, ultimately agreeing to disagree. Working on a project for which I was primarily responsible, she was overdue submitting her portion. I made three follow-up attempts, but she kept putting me off after the initial deadline had come and gone. Obviously, she had many other pressing matters, but had I become too sympathetic to her other responsibilities? Couldn't she work through lunch and add an extra hour for a few days? The project ended up being a couple weeks late and I was irritated about the lack of support. If I did it over, I would have saved myself a lot of aggravation by telling her on my second follow-up, "If you're not able to complete this in the next two days, I'm going to need to turn it in. If they ask me why there's a gap, I'll say they need to ask why your schedule prevented you from fulfilling the assignment" (see: "Two Strikes Allowed"). *Note: For me to have editorialized on why she hadn't finished the task would have been inappropriate, since there may have been a legitimate reason for not making it a priority. That said, she should have accounted for her actions.* This approach would have made me look a little weak, but it would have been better than turning the rest of the report in both late and incomplete. We're still good friends because our relationship is based on mutual respect, even though in this instance from very early in our careers we didn't agree on priorities. When you're tactfully forthright with a peer, it may prevent further incidents when their participation is needed.

Some of this might apply to parenting. I read an article from Bethany Mandel where she begins with the statement, "It's time to make 'parent' a verb again."[44] Mothers and fathers will be more successful raising educated, well-mannered, and socially-conscious children if they see their role as coach and mentor rather than best friend. Guide children in their decisions and explain the possible outcomes, but don't protect them from the natural consequences of their actions if they're not so severe as to be regrettable.

WHY APOLOGIZE?

Even if you're only a little wrong and you know there's a distinct possibility that the other person will never express regret or share fault, apologize. Saying you're sorry cleans the slate and makes you feel better than if you shoulder the burden of pretending to be flawless. This can be done by simply stating, "I got that wrong."

Although I've offered examples when we should make final decisions ourselves, doing so should be the exception. If failure is the result of a group effort, as a team leader we must evaluate the outcome and determine why the poor performance resulted, whether individually or collectively. If there is fault to be borne for a less than satisfactory outcome, an apology is in order. Acknowledgement of remorse is also appropriate if you're answering to another work unit or individual that was negatively impacted.

Don't embrace the pretense of being perfect (see: "Chip on Our Shoulder?"). None of us are. A notable percentage of people in business won't say they're sorry, admit they misspoke, or concede that they made an error or a bad decision. This is interesting considering that most people

---

[44] Mandel, Bethany. "Perspective: Make 'parent' a verb again." *Deseret News*. 18 November 2022. deseret.com/2022/11/18/23466799/free-range-parenting-feral-mara-doemland-lenore-skenazy. Accessed 11 April 2023.

admire those who acknowledge their mistakes much more than those who put themselves on a pedestal and won't come down. If you don't believe this, poll your coworkers and see which type of person they prefer. Then ask why they would rather work with that personality. To further help you accept the benefits of this approach, consider relationships you've had where someone has wronged you but never expressed regret. Then consider individuals who've insulted or injured you, but later expressed sorrow. If you're anything like me, you'd much rather associate with people who are self-correcting and don't pride themselves as being infallible. It's not often easy to apologize, but we must keep striving.

On the other side of the equation, if someone comes to you to apologize, don't rub salt in the wound. They're trying to promote healing between you. Does saying "I told you so" or "Yes, you really made a mess of that" lead to a better long-term outcome?

The need to express regret can often be avoided by not arguing. Somewhere I've heard a proverb that states, "Let arguments fly out open windows."[45] My wife has always refused to argue with me. During the early years of our marriage, I wanted to get to the crux of the matter when we had a difference of opinions. Partially because I enjoyed debating in school, my belief was that whoever could make the most thoughtful case for their opinion should prevail. She would state that she didn't want to discuss the matter with me and would leave the room. Left alone, I would start considering the merits of my wife's side of the disagreement more objectively. This helped me drop barriers and abandon my brash approach. Inevitably, I would realize I needed to apologize.

A final thought: If you find it necessary to ask for forgiveness recurrently, there's a good chance that the root cause needs to be

---

[45] Covey, Stephen R. *The 7 Habits of Highly Effective People: Powerful Lessons in Personal Change.* Free Press, 1989. Chapter 11. In Covey's book, he similarly heard a form of the proverb within advice from his father and applied it to empathetic listening and resolution.

addressed. If you can't make matters better after a couple earnest efforts, don't dismiss the idea to involve professional counseling. There are so many challenges in life where it saves time and frustration to engage an expert, whether medical, financial, technical, or otherwise. Why be hesitant to seek help in treating one of our most valuable assets, our personality and temperament?

CREATE BRIDGES, NOT ENEMIES

In an anecdote about President Abraham Lincoln, he was criticized by a woman for speaking in kind terms about the Confederates. She wanted to know how he could be so generous toward his enemies when he should be seeking to destroy them. In characteristic fashion, Lincoln revealed his wisdom: "Why, madam, do I not destroy my enemies when I make them my friends?"[46]

Dealing with enemies consumes a lot of energy, so don't make any unless there are no other acceptable options. Meet new coworkers more than halfway since first impressions are often wrong (see: "Smile and be Approachable"). Think of how often you've heard of a married couple who said the first time they met they weren't interested or impressed. If we try to work with someone we initially dislike, most of the time we come to understand they're a much better partner than we initially assumed.

Likewise, there's wisdom in the adage, "You attract more flies with honey than vinegar."[47] An example might be confronting a vendor who's

---

[46] This oft-repeated and perhaps apocryphal anecdote has been attributed over time to both President Abraham Lincoln and Holy Roman Emperor Sigismund of Luxembourg.

[47] Though phrasing may vary, this adage was first recorded in Benjamin Franklin's *Poor Richard 1744: An Almanack For the Year of Christ 1744* (Richard Saunders, 1744, founders.archives.gov/documents/Franklin/01-02-02-0100). The adage originally reads: "Tart Words make no Friends: a spoonful of honey will catch more flies than a Gallon of Vinegar."

done a poor job completing one aspect of their commission. If we confront them and accuse them of incompetence or trying to cheat us, they'll be unwilling to expand resources to correct the problem, or at the very least will do so grudgingly. We're more likely to gain cooperation if we sincerely compliment them on what they did complete correctly, before asking them to fix a portion of the job that doesn't quite match up to the quality of the rest of their execution.

Pick your battles carefully. Don't use up political capital on little things. There was once a situation when a member of a marketing department's leadership team marched into a senior executive's office and argued for forty-five minutes over a word the executive had changed in promotional material. The word escapes me, but in this situation, it was splitting hairs without any legal or regulatory ramifications. It was just a battle of semantics. How could the executive not help but be annoyed and wonder if this individual was equally disagreeable performing the rest of his job description?

If you're defensive by nature, when someone starts firing questions at you, buy time and goodwill by responding with something to the effect of, "That's a good question" (see: "Chip on Our Shoulder?"). Next, interact in a thoughtful and responsive way. Perhaps you can ask for time to thoroughly research the details if the issue is unclear or complex.

Accept and support the group consensus unless it's morally wrong and violates your creed. If called for, begin by carefully assessing whether the action is beyond your control (preventing you from applying a remedy) and so egregious that you don't want to be associated with it in any way. If you know something is important and right, be willing to stand up for it while being sure your principles aren't pretentious. *Note: On sporadic occasions, I was just looking for something to violate my principles and my bias was based on a lack of knowledge.* If it's a very serious matter, ask yourself if there are other reasons why you don't want to continue in this job? This is a very personal question. Before quitting, be certain the practice is morally objectionable. Keep in mind that if you become unreasonably critical, there aren't many flawless companies out there. You could always try to start one, but realize that it might not pass everyone else's scrutiny either.

When I was talking my way onto the management group for one retail firm, I sat with one of the owners as we worked to understand one another. At one point in reaction to some conjectural concerns I said, "You can always count on me to do my job well. However, should there come a time when I morally disagree with a corporate directive or practice, I'll come to you and tell you I can't support that direction. I recognize that this isn't my company, and if I'm not able to talk you out of it, then I need to go my way. But on the other hand, you need to be fair in recognizing the contributions I've made so I'm not hurt while securing another position." While that situation was never even closely approached, this accord served as the foundation to my employment at that company.

Give your full attention to the person in front of you. Ram Dass advised, "Don't think about the future. Just be here now. Don't think about the past. Just be here now."[48] If you're at home with your spouse and they need to talk, put down your smartphone and listen. This isn't something I've totally mastered, but you can learn from my mistakes. Relationships are built on concern and communication. One of the fastest ways to make an enemy is to ignore someone and act like they don't matter.

Don't verbally or emotionally punish people for reporting the unvarnished truth. Similarly, don't accuse someone of misrepresentation unless you've verified the details in a fair and reliable manner. Not only will people resent how you treat them, but they'll also withhold information in the future to avoid interacting with us as much as possible. In that same light, statements like "Just fix the problem" are another way of saying, "Don't confuse me with the facts" or "I really don't care about you or how challenging this is to accomplish."

Avoid absolutes most of the time. Leave room for a somewhat gracious

---

[48] Dass, Ram. *Be Here Now*. Harmony/Rodale, 1971. pp. 90.

exit. Even if you think you're right, say "If my memory serves me correctly," "To the best of my knowledge," or "I'm fairly sure." If instead you come across with, "How much do you want to bet?" or "I know for a fact," it will eventually catch up with you when you're wrong and off you'll come from the pedestal you created for yourself. Coworkers remember when this happens and won't be quick to forgive your arrogance. Be a little flexible. It doesn't always have to be exactly your way.

DON'T TURN A POSITIVE INTO A NEGATIVE

We usually only witness a small percentage of what an employee does while carrying out their duties. Out of a forty-five-hour work week, how many hours are we physically with them observing their behavior? Sometimes the brief moments we do see can be misinterpreted.

Allow me to illustrate by sharing an experience I had while working as an assistant buyer in the stereo department at a downtown flagship store. One day, the commissioned sales staff took it upon themselves to correct some long overdue concerns regarding the merchandise presentation in their area. Normally this task should have been handled by a stock team working before or after store hours. The store manager, whose name I can't recall, had a standing rule that no hand trucks or large carts should be on the sales floor during hours when the store was open to the public. Working all day between assisting customers, the team reorganized and moved almost all of the audio merchandise without using any of the banned equipment. However, the final task required one load on a furniture float (a large, flat, four-wheeled cart on which you place items like a sofa) to move some heavy non-essential display racks to a distant stockroom. As luck would have it, the general manager walked off the elevator only to come face to face with an unattended load of stereo-related furniture. When the salespeople showed up just a few seconds later he reprimanded them royally. These employees, who weren't allowed to work outside of store hours, had gone the extra mile to perform a task that had been neglected by the stockroom staff for at least a month. Leaving unnecessary and bulky cabinets out in the reworked sales display was a much greater offense than the quick run to the stockroom with a furniture float. A positive was turned into a negative. At least for the rest of my six months in that assignment, the staff never again lifted a finger to fix any display problems. Instead of being praised and then kindly reminded about the rule's intent, they just got chewed out.

Another instance involved a luncheon we held for the warehouse staff in a distribution facility, which totaled over 300 people. Prior to the event, we calculated how many coworkers were assigned to the second shift and set aside generous food portions for them. The first shift had plenty to eat. When the second shift staff broke for their evening meal, the men beat the women to the lunch line (gentlemen, please) and made Dagwood sandwiches (up to an inch of lunch meat on their individual hoagies). One of the supervisors called me at home and described the problem, so we opened the cafeteria refrigerators for the women and more polite men to have enough meat and cheese. A few days later, two of the female staff ran into the owner while shopping at the flagship store and complained about the problem. Of course, I heard about it soon thereafter. My natural inclination was to not have any more luncheons and simply eliminate the source of the complaint. Unfortunately, that would have penalized non-complainers as well. I shared my viewpoint and logic with the two unhappy coworkers and they grasped the issue. Their feedback was welcome so we could improve subsequent events. Yet, by running it up the chain of command before we had an opportunity to respond, they made a beneficial effort appear detrimental which could have discouraged any future attempts.

One final story: while working at one retail company we determined to run our own fleet of tractor-trailers to stores in neighboring states, as opposed to contracting with a third-party trucking firm to perform that service. The exact amount has escaped me, but it annually saved over ten thousand dollars for every store involved. Prior to making the change, we shared the analysis with the senior manager overseeing buying for the entire company. Since the expense was part of her gross margin calculation, she rightfully wanted to ensure it was an actual savings. We accommodated her request the first time, but it became tedious to go over the same analysis with her two additional times. Clearly her trust level was low, but I didn't comprehend why.

After the program had been in place about six months, one of our drivers experienced a medical condition (I'm pretty sure it was kidney stones). He called and asked if he could return home without making one of the deliveries loaded on the trailer he was pulling. Permission was granted. We didn't have another driver available, so the plan was to cross-dock the load onto a third-party carrier's truck for a rescheduled delivery. This would cost around $750. When the VP learned of the delayed delivery, she called to ask the plan. When we explained, her response focused on concern with the extra expense and whether we were going to charge the extra fees to her gross margin, since this wasn't her fault. Really? Our program saved her thousands of dollars each month and now when something insignificant happened, we were asked to pay the costs. Perhaps she was just very frugal, but I was frustrated justifying the expense after my team had devised a cost-saving initiative to help both the buying office and the enterprise.

The moral of these stories should be self-explanatory.

TAKING CARE OF CUSTOMERS

Let me set the stage for this chapter by sharing a small pet peeve. Having worked in retail stores for a notable portion of my early career, may I tell you how unimpressive it is to approach the set of double doors at a store entrance and find that one of them is still secured to the door casing's threshold and lintel? A sign stating, "Use other door" doesn't do much to change my feelings. It takes an employee less than thirty seconds to flip both manual lock pins so the door will be open during business hours. Of course, employees have to perform this task all over again at the end of the day, so double that amount of time. Does this tiny inconvenience on the part of a staff member outweigh the convenience of every customer who grabs the wrong door handle, or all of the times patrons converge at the door simultaneously and would appreciate a two-way path? So much for first impressions saying, "Welcome to our place of business, we're excited you chose to visit us" (see: "Influencing Impressions" and "Set Higher Standards").

Occasionally, a Fortune 500 company which understands the value of customers will go to extra lengths to compensate them for any inconvenience caused by their failure. If your car is subject to a recall, would you rather call the dealership half a dozen times to find out when the part has finally arrived (I've experienced this) or have them call you when it arrives and then provide a loaner vehicle or help to transport you to and from work?

As a store manager (the person who often interacts with many of the upset customers), I eventually decided not to explain company policy or constraints until the shopper had been allowed to fully express their dissatisfaction. No disrespect intended, but the first task was to get the steam out of the kettle. This included asking specific questions regarding what they purchased, when the transaction took place, which salesperson helped them, and so on. Only after they'd finished venting and felt understood did I take the next step and ask what they wanted. There was no need to tell them about their options or store policy at this point. If they wanted an exchange and that was within my authority, I would just do it. Maybe they could be salvaged as a patron if they appreciated how swiftly the problem was corrected. If they asked for something I couldn't or wouldn't do—such as fire a highly regarded salesperson on the spot—the next step was to give them their options. This is comparable to letting them look at a menu. If they picked one of the permissible remedies (like a full refund, a credit on their charge card, a store credit, or reordering/locating a replacement item) the challenge was to make it happen as quickly as possible. Then in a clear and simple manner, I would reassure them that any contributing factors to the situation would be addressed (for instance, "I'm going to personally sit with the salesperson and discuss this complaint"). If they didn't like any of the options offered, then my goal was to broker compromise. Utmost effort was given to doing all of this pleasantly, remembering that if the interaction came across as resentful, resources were wasted because the customer was still going to be unsatisfied and shop elsewhere (see: "Our Own Worst Enemy"). *Note: If you're not the person who can solve the customer's problem, don't just tell the patron who to contact. Carry the ball until you can make a firm connection for them to the person who will address their complaint.*

Some workers don't realize that even when they're not identified as part of the sales team, they still have customers for whom they should care. I can't think of a situation where a department in a company doesn't have either internal or external customers they need to satisfy. Research and development (R&D) need to satisfy senior management and stockholders, if publicly held. Operations need to satisfy not only the external customers but also the sales group, and so on. Occasionally, internal customers don't understand constraints and make demands a company can't deliver. When you get a request that you can't fulfill (for instance, giving free shipping to everyone in a recently hit storm area when you would need a software enhancement to sort zip codes), don't just say you can't do it. Tell them the reason why, so they won't misinterpret your attitude.

SECTION FIVE

ETHICS

SPEND GOODWILL, BUT CAREFULLY

Goodwill is more often earned than freely given, notwithstanding individuals who inherently meet others more than halfway. Perhaps in some cases a person will do us a favor because of a friendship they had with one of our family members or friends or just because they're kind. In high school, I experienced this as I followed two older brothers through each grade. They were both all-around athletes and one was senior class president while the other was student body president. Periodically, teachers made kind remarks about them and treated me as though I was also upstanding, even though I didn't always measure up to their example. That said, we should never intentionally put ourselves in a position where we've used up all of the goodwill we've accumulated. We're going to need help from time to time, so it's only proper that we try to return the favor at the next opportunity.

The general manager of a retail distribution center where I was on the management staff had several close associates among the non-exempt staff. He would regularly go down to the cafeteria and eat lunch with and visit them. This created jealousy with some of the management team and other hourly employees not in this circle. I wondered if this would ever backfire on him. It was later revealed that he indeed knew how to handle these relationships when one member of this group received a write-up for attendance.

Immediately following a corrective action discussion with their area manager in the human resource office, the employee marched upstairs to the general manager's office and was overheard saying something like, "I was just given a written warning for attendance. I thought we were friends." His reply was classic: "We are friends, but that doesn't mean you don't have to come to work." It was perfect. Without disavowing their relationship, he made it crystal clear that just because they enjoyed one another's company, he wasn't going to create special guidelines for them or anyone else. Everyone needed to adhere to the rules and, although it remained unspoken, he hoped there weren't ulterior motives for wanting to know him better.

As a member of the leadership team, help maintain the delineation between supervisors, peers, friends, and employees. Communicate it kindly, but clearly, at the first sign of a coworker asking you to ignore the tenets. Work associates can be friends, but everyone needs to be responsible for their conduct and job performance (see: "Two Strikes Allowed"). We all have obligations and commitments that require us to stay employed. When this predicament occurs, humanely but also firmly convey the message, "Please don't ask me to jeopardize my job to cover for your work-related failures."

There have been several occasions when we've hired one of my acquaintances. Almost from day one on the job, a few of them have acted as though they deserved preferential treatment. They wanted to hitch their wagon to someone else's star: mine (though it was a very tiny star). If someone is kind enough to help you land a position, don't make them regret it. To combat this reoccurring issue, one of my directors and I agreed to have an informal policy. Basically, "Who you know will get you an interview. However, once your foot is in the door it's your duty to impress your potential supervisor with your past performance, skills, and abilities if you hope to land the job." Once on the job, any benefactor of outside relationships must be coached into recognizing that they need to be self-reliant moving forward.

Take for example a time I was at another West Coast firm and we had a new employee come to the distribution center on a short-term assignment. He was very arrogant and unconcerned about our issues supporting some of his outlandish service requests. He didn't want to listen to our staff, let alone try to address their apprehensions or suggestions to help move his project forward. After his motives became clearer, I said, "You know, you're not trying very hard to work with our team." To this he replied, "I don't really care about those people. All I care about is pleasing my uncle [an executive of the company]." The good news was that his time with the business was brief. He ended up quitting after about six months, perhaps because he'd incorrectly planned on experiencing a career fast-track due to his connection.

As a subordinate, if you're connected to someone important others on the job may already know it. If you say something, it's announcing that you want an unacceptable career short-cut and want to get ahead through unfair means. Similarly, if you work with a relative avoid the adverse undertones of nepotism by exhibiting decent behavior. When my oldest son and I worked together, several peers were surprised to learn about our relationship even after several years (it helped that he was blessed with his good looks from my wife's side of the family). We used to discreetly go on walks at lunch and neither of us advertised that we were related. We both wanted to succeed on our own merits and tried not to intrude in the other's career, feeling it would only be a negative for those working with us.

Consider other relationships besides your own. Criticizing or poorly treating another person's friend will in turn hurt your friendship with them. You may not care about your rapport with the person you're disparaging, but your comments may get back to them and make matters worse. Moreover, their friend might find it necessary to defend them and align against you, either out of loyalty or because of the bias you exhibited.

WILLING TO FORGIVE

Unfortunately, I can recall numerous things I wish I could undo. When I had to find another job because I said something impulsive to my boss, I moved away and left my cousin who was still living and working in the Bay Area. Several months later, his three-year-old daughter was diagnosed with cancer. If I'd known that earlier, I could have bit my tongue so I didn't find it necessary to resign, then I could have been a better support to his family. Without a crystal ball, we never know how things will transpire and so we have all the more reason to try to avoid regrettable missteps.

On multiple occasions, I expressed to my cousin how badly I felt. Being a wonderful human being, he told me he realized we didn't know this trial was going to happen and he didn't hold any bad feelings. Because of this, I'm trying harder to forgive those who periodically step on my toes, or worse.

To help bring this concept home, allow another personal experience. My wife and I had a daughter who was chronically ill. We spent over a year getting her correctly diagnosed and sometimes she wouldn't be able to make it to school or church. We had a neighbor who led the children's part of our congregation. One day my wife had to call her and asked to be excused from a teaching assignment because our daughter suddenly became too sick to leave home. Later the neighbor said, "I didn't know one of your little girls had health problems." Only a few months earlier, we'd spent twenty minutes telling her about our struggle to get her condition identified, but she simply didn't remember. My wife and I discussed this and decided that it wasn't everyone else's job to carry our burdens. We were going to do our best to be grateful when someone reached out, did us a kindness, or took an interest in our challenges. This is the better option, as opposed to feeling sorry for ourselves when somebody missed a chance to help us with a problem that weighs us down. Try to appreciate things people do for you as opposed to assuming others know exactly what we need and when we want it done. Rather, learn to focus on and be grateful for compassion. Other people such as neighbors, family, friends, or coworkers aren't going to be there for us every time we need it, just like we won't be there for them every time they need it. Expecting this from life will leave us disillusioned. It's thought that Abraham Lincoln once said, "Most people are about as happy as they make their minds up to be."[49] We'll end up miserable if we think everyone is assigned to be our constant guardian angels.

TAKE THE HIGH ROAD

Ethics are often a by-product of motivation. Individual motivation can be characterized by four different scenarios.

First, an individual can do the wrong things for the wrong reasons. This could come in the form of blaming someone for a mistake they didn't make to eliminate them as competition for an upcoming promotion. When the truth finally comes to light, it reveals the perpetrator as subversive, devious, self-serving, or counterproductive. Most coworkers won't want anything to do with this kind of character and are unwilling to help them if they can avoid it.

Second, those who do the wrong things for the right reasons. This could include someone lying about who came up with a great concept in order to credit a friend they feel deserves a break, but consequently disregarding the person who originated the idea because they're consistently getting recognized for their achievements. This might make the person spreading

---

[49] Variations of this saying have been attributed to Abraham Lincoln by Frank Crane, Orison Swett Marden (*How to Get What You* Want, Thomas Y. Crowell Co., 1917), and the film *Pollyanna* (1960).

the lie look somewhat well-intentioned, but ultimately also insensitive and dishonest. Most peers will still try to avoid the untruthful employee, even if they sympathize with their motives. It becomes obvious they're a poor decision maker and a hindrance to group progress. The employee will soon be on their own, since coworkers and superiors will grow tired of them misrepresenting the facts. Being well-meaning counts for very little in this scenario, but at least people in this group aren't considered as bad as the snakes in the previous group.

Third, people who do the right things for the wrong reasons. For instance, volunteering to serve on a special project team so you can garner as much credit as possible. You guessed it: no one wants to work with this person in these situations either. They have no sympathy since it's obvious they're self-serving. Superiors may initially look past the complaints they get from coworkers because the subordinate is helping advance the venture in some manner. But eventually it's going to be hard—if not impossible—for this bad actor to get things accomplished as any team support they had fades away.

Lastly, a person who does the right things for the right reasons. These individuals volunteer to serve on that special project team because the effort will contribute to company profit and efficiency. This should always be our course of action, however, don't be surprised if some people resent your success because they're suspicious. Let's face it, this behavior can resemble doing the right things for the wrong reasons because you and your team might reap recognition in the process. If you encounter jealousy or resentment, the best defense is to explain your purpose in terms of principled objectives. In this case, you're able to sincerely articulate your actions if confronted.

It's even better if your coworkers choose to defend your character and intentions. Remember to give as much genuine praise as possible and they might occasionally affirm your contribution (see: "Give the Credit to the Team"). Other than overtly reporting results on a regular basis, be hesitant to become your own public relations department. It's better to have someone else fill that role. The more you promote yourself, the less inclined anyone else will be to mention your achievements. They'll figure you've done a thorough job patting yourself on the back without any help from them. A by-product of self-endorsement—and sometimes even team-endorsement—is that too often it makes your boss think of your weaknesses (which include your ego) in an attempt to balance the scales. The exception to this rule might be when you encounter an outright misrepresentation of truth. If it becomes necessary to set the record straight, do so calmly from the perspective of a team member clarifying the particulars and appropriately crediting others involved.

After weighing the various options, isn't doing the right things for the right reasons the more noble path? Remember, your peers will check you and make sure your walk matches your talk. If you're caught taking credit for others' work or claiming results that can't be substantiated, they'll call you out, if not to your face, then behind your back.

Be aware that if someone spreads disinformation or unflattering observations about you, it's ill advised to ramp it up and return the favor. You'll both be guilty. Whenever you get in the gutter, it seldom helps improve matters if you feel you had a good reason to end up there (see: "Chip on Our Shoulder?" and "Create Bridges, Not Enemies").

SQUEAKY CLEAN

At one company, a man who oversaw quality took some samples that were suspiciously clean of microorganisms to a third party to see if they'd been irradiated by the vendor, an unacceptable method of treatment at his firm. Unfortunately, he failed to sign out the samples and ended up being terminated amid accusations he had taken them to a competitor. Because I'd known and worked with him earlier, I never believed he was guilty of the greater crime but his failure to follow established procedures left him exposed.

On another occasion, a woman I knew accepted a job offer where I'd recently been hired. She was going to be a second-shift production manager and work in a different facility, but live near us to facilitate socializing. My wife and I were excited for her family to be joining us in the area. We were only there for a couple more years before I left to accept a job from the senior manager who recruited me and had moved on to another venture. A while later, we learned my acquaintance had lost her job. She was apparently on the late shift one evening after the general manager had gone home. Someone from corporate human resources had brought by the approved reviews for the managerial staff and requested that they be placed on the GM's desk. Curiosity got the best of my friend and she peeked at her review. She then told another manager she trusted about how to access the packet and his own evaluation. The other manager got further carried away and surveyed all of the reviews. Soon thereafter, he passed along confidential information to others. Ultimately, it came to the attention of senior leadership. An investigation began to determine how this material was compromised. Even though she had very strong performance ratings, a company policy was violated and both managers were dismissed. I'm certain it wasn't easy being unemployed with a small family and without many resources. She went on to be very successful and never made that mistake again.

My offering is that we should never give anyone an easy excuse to fire us. If we take pens home, bring them back. If we get a travel advance, return every cent of the unaccounted funds. If we accidently use our corporate credit card for a personal purchase, pay it back and get a receipt as soon as humanly possible. Refuse to fudge on mileage or anything else of that nature.

We had a supervisor on second shift invite some male entertainers to a Nevada warehouse one evening. I suppose she wanted to impress these performers she'd apparently met at a local club with the scope of her responsibilities. After a short tour of the facility, they ended up in a conference room. Several other members of the supervisory staff and a few select friends were invited to party. Things got a little out of control. The guys, while not totally disrobing, were encouraged to get up on the conference table and show off their dance routines. When the event came to light, several individuals were terminated, particularly those in supervisory roles and those who perpetrated the episode. Others were given final warnings. The interesting thing is that several of them said they knew it was wrong, but they stayed and participated anyway. One employee had the common sense and courage to leave. That person wasn't placed on any kind of warning.

A peer you consider a friend might take advantage of your good nature and miss deadlines or assignments, impacting your job performance or perhaps worse. Perhaps they have an assignment as part of the team you're leading. When this happens, you need to maintain a healthy separation between your friendship and your business relationship (see: "Seek Respect Before Friendship" and "Spend Goodwill, but Carefully"). Don't regularly cover for people just because they're not conscientious enough to put in a few extra hours to complete their assignment. If you choose to absorb some blame the first time an offender drops the ball, be sure to avoid reoccurrences by having a private heart-to-heart conversation so they know you'll opt not to cover for them going forward (see: "Micromanage Non-Performers"). For one thing, your workers need to speak up if they have too many projects on their plate (see: "Overwhelming To-Do Lists"). The main point is to not engage in any unacceptable behavior, like breaking policies or procedures for someone else.

In a similar vein, two of my acquaintances (a woman and a man) were working as district sales managers for a furniture manufacturer headquartered in the Southeast. They both lost their jobs because they signed expense reports for another district manager who was misrepresenting entries. My friends had the authority to sign these reports for those who reported up, but this group of leaders all needed to get their expenses approved by their regional manager. The exact nature of the problem was never shared with me, but I could guess the abuser either didn't have receipts or padded and fabricated expenses. The other countersigners weren't inspecting receipts closely enough when approving his forms. The abuser was fired for stealing from the company. My contacts were let go for allowing it to happen, not that it makes much difference when you lose your livelihood.

The easiest way to avoid this is to say no the first time you're approached about doing something outside of guidelines. Just say it straight, "I can't approve that, you know you need to run it past the boss," or whatever else clarifies your intention to follow protocol. If you do find yourself in a compromising situation (like the person who left the party in the conference room), get out ASAP. It may save you.

GIVE THE CREDIT TO THE TEAM

A coach's performance is judged by how well the team performs, not on how much credit they claim. There were several instances in the early years of the NBA when a great player near retirement age became the "player-coach," meaning he functioned in both roles. Generally, I don't think this strategy proved to be an overwhelming success. For one thing, who benches the coach when he can't guard his man or when he keeps missing ill-advised shots? In the post-game interview, what hat does he wear? If he brags about the 30 points he made, how do the other players feel about their leader? Does the owner care about what kind of statistics the player-coach puts up if he starts playing less but the team does well in the playoffs?

As I'm writing this chapter I think of Jerry Sloan, who retired after coaching the Chicago Bulls and then the Utah Jazz for 26 years combined. He frequently declared that the team's failure was his responsibility but he used few, if any, more typical inspirational techniques. He expected the members of his team to motivate themselves because they were professionals and handsomely paid. Karl Malone said of Sloan's coaching style, "He wants you to come, work hard, do what he tells you to do.... Me and him clash every now and then, but it's one of those things in the end where I want what he wants—to win."[50] When a game was won (1,221 of them, to be exact), you never heard Coach Sloan take credit for calling the game-saving play.[51] On the other hand, he would acknowledge but not lavish the contributions of the players who made notable efforts positively impacting the resulting win. No one got kudos if they lost regardless of their personal effort because after all, they lost.

There are times when the universe doesn't align with what is right and honorable. Regardless, the better way to proceed in the long run is to give credit to your team. They're more apt to embrace you and your role for doing so. Likewise, if your business unit is successful, the more your superiors will appreciate the leadership you provide. Even if you don't personally score the points, the powers that be won't want to take the risk of replacing you with someone else who may not be able to keep the team as happy, successful, and productively engaged.

Some tasks are best performed by team leaders. Don't delegate everything. Furthermore, avoid putting yourself on a pedestal and limit chastising anyone working under your direction unless it's truly warranted. Very early on in my career while working in Minnesota, I recall a holiday gathering where everyone in attendance received a reprimand from an executive because someone else on the program said, "Happy Holidays" instead of "Merry Christmas." Ironically, a few days later many who had been in attendance received a Christmas card from the executive's family

---

[50] Goldstein, Richard. "Jerry Sloan, Hall of Fame N.B.A. Guard and Coach, Dies at 78." *The New York Times*. 22 May 2020.

[51] Goldstein, Richard. "Jerry Sloan, Hall of Fame N.B.A. Guard and Coach, Dies at 78." *The New York Times*. 22 May 2020.

signed "Happy Holidays." No one is perfect, it's just that those who believe they're flawless will end up being resented. If you claim to be perfect, everyone will watch and wait to see you violate your own pronouncement (see: "Would You Follow Someone like Yourself?," "Walking the Walk," and "Why Apologize?").

GOOD HUMOR ONLY

The best person to make a joke about is yourself. My father was charmingly self-deprecating. He would say stuff like, "They kicked me out of fifth grade because I'd been there so many years, I started shaving." People were drawn to and admired him because he wasn't trying to shine a spotlight on himself. They liked him and knew that he was competent. He didn't have to become a walking resume, always sharing his accomplishments to impress others. A little of this rubbed off on me, but not nearly enough.

If you ever meet me, you'll recognize immediately that I'm not a handsome guy. Among other things I'm 6'5", lanky, and bald. To try and break down barriers with people, I'll joke about myself because I'm comfortable in my skin. This is partially because my childhood buddies and I—some of whom I still see frequently—have kidded each other about our imperfections for as far back as I can remember.

On the flip side, I take minor offense to having someone joke about the appearance of my friends or family when they haven't known them very long. In my opinion, they haven't earned the right or paid their dues yet in demonstrating that they're a friend or ally.

As a rule, don't let people make off-color comments or degrading remarks about one another. Joke to somebody's strength. Avoid teasing another person about something which might make them self-conscious. Allow another personal story: one of my bosses chewed his fingernails. To stop this habit, he applied clear nail polish to his fingertips. I recall him

CONCEPTS OF MANAGING

telling me that it had a bitter taste to discourage the practice. One morning I walked into his office when he was alone. I asked if I could borrow some of the polish. He said, "Do you chew your nails?" "No," I said, "I just want to put some on my back side, so you'll stop chewing on it." I'd believed it was clever enough to make him laugh. He didn't. I suppose I could have made matters even worse and cracked the joke in our daily manager meeting, but even in private it was an insensitive comment.

Generally now, after having some of my edges rubbed off, if I tease someone it's often a sign of affection. When doing so, I try to only tease about their strong points. However, even that gets misinterpreted. One of the times I served as store manager, I teased one of the fun-loving trainees in return for some good-natured grief he was giving me. In response to one of his jabs, I said something about letting him go if he didn't start showing a little more respect (his position with the company was very secure because he was a solid, above average performer). Well, you guessed it. In less than an hour it had spread through the whole store that I intended to fire him. Remember that much of the population interprets remarks very literally. Joking apparently wasn't something that some of the staff engaged in with either their families or friends.

Here's additional evidence. During our early marriage, my wife and I lived in the same neighborhood as an acquaintance of one of my sisters-in-law. One day I came home with a bag full of vegetables picked from my brother's garden, after being invited to do so anytime I wanted. When I happened upon my sister-in-law's friend, she asked about my bag full of bounty. I joked, "Oh, it's just some vegetables I stole out of my brother's garden." Guess who turned me in? Of course, my brother just laughed when my supposed misdeeds were reported. But remember the point: know your audience and be sure they know you.

Telling suggestive jokes or making politically incorrect statements will eventually come back to haunt you. While living in Pennsylvania, a truck driver for whom I was ultimately responsible, came within an inch of losing his job for telling a dirty joke to staff members at a store's receiving department. The committee who reviewed the complaint placed him on a first and final warning. In a different time and place, he may have been fired on the spot. When I questioned him about it, he said he'd done it before and no one seemed to mind. He thought they were okay with the nature of his conversation. I strongly suggested that he never risk that again since he couldn't be 100% positive that his audience wouldn't be offended at some point in time. It was clear he had made a bad choice. Besides, dirty jokes have no redeeming value.

A SHORT HARASSMENT POLICY

Sexual harassment is against federal law, but other types of harassment should also be a violation of written company policy so you can discipline and correct any type of bullying or inappropriate conduct. Federal laws make it illegal for your company to deny employment, harass, demote, terminate, or pay less. It's illegal to treat someone less favorably because of race, color, religion, sex, sexual orientation, gender identity, national origin, disability, or status as a protected veteran. It's also illegal to engage in retaliation. I would add my view that any additional identifier, including things such as physical appearance or mannerisms, should be added to this list. In some ways, harassment policies should be as simple as saying, "Don't harass for any reason." The more examples you give, sometimes the more clarification some employees want.

As mentioned in the previous chapter, I had a driver who told dirty jokes to receiving personnel at a store until one woman felt he stepped over the line (see: "Good Humor Only"). His defense was that it used to be okay with her. Part of my unsympathetic response included, "If you never tell filthy stories, you'll never have to worry about where that line is anymore now, will you?"

Understand that when someone comes to you and says they want to relate something regarding harassment in confidence, you must be careful in your reply. Indicate that you will do whatever is possible to maintain their anonymity, but that your job responsibilities require you to make certain that violations of company policy are reported and addressed if necessary. Then encourage the complainant to share their concern so that situation can be improved. *Note: Too often when approached in this manner, a manager will agree (in advance of understanding the predicament) not to disclose any details and then to their dismay discover the allegation is very serious and should be dealt with and not swept under the rug.*

When you get into a "she said, he said" situation that can't be validated and isn't an offense that requires immediate termination, put a stake in the ground for the protection of the complainant. A young man with whom I worked was accused of brushing up against a woman from behind in a crowded group, and it made her wonder if it was more than incidental contact. Although the HR manager couldn't validate the incident, he had a conversation with the young man anyway. HR wanted the employee to be on notice for numerous reasons: (a) to protect the victim from a repeat of the offense; (b) to let the victim see that something was being done to address the matter, even if they hoped for more punitive action; (c) to make the accused (guilty or innocent) aware there had been a complaint; (d) to protect the company by addressing the incident; and finally, (e) to facilitate swift and decisive action if any other validating complaints were ever made. *Note: Regardless of personal feelings, set them aside and honor and carry out company protocol.*

My training in this area mandates that HR should partner with us in pulling the accused individual aside to inform them of the charge of wrongdoing. Next, explain that this is going in their file (if it never happened again, it would most likely become a forgotten piece of paper). The employee must then be told that retaliation, or even unnecessary contact, is not tolerated. Any further complaints will be more condemning because there will then be either two people or two instances to corroborate the conduct. To protect itself legally, the company's next course will most likely be termination. I was involved with a group of department heads reviewing an issue where a man had repeated an offense (trying to steal a kiss) against a second coworker and was immediately dismissed.

A final comment: don't remain silent on the topic with your staff. At your very next opportunity, give the simple yet clear advice to your team members that harassment of any type isn't condoned if they wish to maintain employment. Cover the illegal harassment categories, including any others expanded by corporate policy. Furthermore, instruct your supervisory staff to be diligent in monitoring and reporting any policy violations. Remind them regularly of the expectation that they should be proactive in efforts to keep a positive standard alive in the operation's culture.

SECTION SIX

ODDS & ENDS

MULTI-TASKING: VIRTUE OR VICE?

Are you amazed how much time it takes non-performers to wade through small tasks and assignments? While the concept "be here now" I advocated earlier from spiritual leader Ram Dass has its place, there are many situations where multi-tasking is beneficial.[52] This is especially true if we're not in the midst of a one-on-one discussion or interaction with a small group. The struggle with multi-tasking is knowing when we should and should not employ it. If I'm working on a project or urgent email and an employee comes into my office, I have a hard time yielding my full attention on a dime. This is clearly not the time to be dividing my concentration between conversation with a staff member and another pressing matter. I need to either schedule to meet with them after completing this pressing assignment or, if their problem merits undivided consideration, place whatever I was working on aside. But this isn't a valid reason to abandon multitasking entirely. Say you're in a large meeting like a seminar and the presentation is content-poor or a rehash of something you've heard previously; it can be very helpful to discretely turn our attention to another task that's on the horizon.

---

[52] Dass, Ram. *Be Here Now*. Harmony/Rodale, 1971. pp. 50

Make easy things happen quickly (see: "Become the Go-To Person"). When a staff member finishes sharing their legitimate concerns (not a complaint about another person) and I determine someone else needs to be notified, I hope the employee appreciates the sense of urgency exhibited when I place a phone call or send an email or text while we're still together.

There's an old proverb, "Well begun is half done." If we have an assignment, the sooner you can turn some thought to it—even briefly—the better. This figuratively raises our antenna so that anything relevant heard going forward can now be added to our knowledge banks (see: "Planting Seeds"). It also affords us time to mull things over while waiting for an appointment, standing in line, or involved in other mundane activities. Perhaps you're giving a presentation in two weeks and you sat down now and outlined the essence of what ought to be covered. I guarantee that additional worthwhile ideas will come to your mind before the actual event. If you make it a point to record these periodic reflections as they arise, your material will be more interesting. Applying this practice in addressing challenges allows you to identify input that relates to the issue, recognize opportunities to have impromptu discussions with others, and weigh various options that might be employed. This also helps avoid the stress of leaving something until the last minute. The old expression "You can kill two birds with one stone" is even more relevant today with the amount of information and tasks we're required to process.

If others will be involved in a joint venture or project, sharing an early heads-up allows them the same luxury. The sooner they can give attention to a distant deadline, the more opportunities along the way you provide for the entire team to be successful.

Don't become so myopic that you must stick with one task until it's done before focusing on the next one. Of course, if the undertaking is urgent and you're up against a hard deadline, this would be an exception. Otherwise, survey your to-do list and balance what is important, what can be delegated swiftly, what needs to be communicated soon, and what you can knock off the list along the way. Don't just start working on the first item that grabs your attention (see: "Was it the Assignment Given?"). Don't set off to accomplish an errand without contemplating if you can accomplish something else in the process (see: "Earn More Than We're Paid"). Take advantage of chance meetings with coworkers, travel patterns, and the like. On your way down to the first floor to drop a package in the mail, you can swing by purchasing and see if they've placed that order you need to go out today. Since you're also near accounting, you can submit the invoice you just approved and ask a staff member when the monthly reports will be available. Like the carnival performer spinning plates on poles, get as many things going as rapidly as possible and then keep things moving by coming back periodically to add some energy to the effort. If you focus on just one plate, the rest quickly lose their momentum and fall and break on the floor.

WHEN AND HOW TO NEGOTIATE

When I completed grad school, I had three job offers in retail, my field of choice. Offer A was with a department store headquartered nearby. They offered me an hourly rate (seriously, hourly) that worked out to be less than I was making while working my way through school managing the men's department at a smaller department store. Offers B and C were for two out-of-state companies with identical salaries. After visiting these two, decision time came. Both companies were informed that I had other comparable offers and that I was weighing my options in the next day or two. My contact from Company B made it clear that I could be easily replaced with comments like, "There are many other candidates who will gladly take your place" if I didn't select them. Company C made it clear that they wanted me very much and offered me an additional 18%. Guess where I ended up? It wasn't entirely because of the salary—I wanted to be wanted.

Timing is a critical element of any negotiation, but I want to address how it relates to your compensation package. The best time to negotiate is when you're taking a new job or accepting a promotion or assignment change. Leadership has decided you're the right person because you're at your "showroom best." A maintenance manager I oversaw in California was terrific at getting projects done and running a tight ship. On multiple occasions when it was time to do reviews, a couple of my colleagues approached me wanting to be sure that I dinged him for one little thing or another that bothered them (I never could determine why they were so interested in his livelihood). They even wanted me to tell him he wasn't promotable, because he lacked a degree or the necessary polish. Funnily enough, when it was time to advance someone from his peer group, company-wide, to be responsible for all of the other maintenance departments in the logistics organization, the search committee couldn't rave about him enough. He got a substantial increase and this became the springboard for the rest of his career. He was the right person for the job when opportunity came knocking. This illustrates how at the right moment in time, a person's stock can significantly increase, changing the whole dynamic of negotiation (see: "Over Prepared").

If an employer feels you're a match, those making the hiring decision want your acceptance soon so they can move on to other challenges. Like a boss once told me, "They won't hire you unless they need you." After taking the job, expect to roll up your sleeves and begin an immediate assessment of the area assigned to you, closely followed by implementing the appropriate solutions (see: "Handling a Crisis").

When interviewing at an outside firm, don't be caught off guard if you're asked in your first interview about your existing or previous compensation, especially from an action-oriented senior manager. A red flag goes up for me when I ask for wage or salary, and I get an answer like, "Around $80,000 a year." If the candidate can't be forthcoming about this, I worry I won't be able to get a straight answer later after they come on board. I need to establish mutual trust and respect if this relationship moves forward. Besides, I need to formulate an offer that will be fair and attractive. That doesn't mean candidates can't stand pat for the financial package they require.

When you interview with a prospective employer, let them bring up compensation first. Once broached, don't get so carried away talking about it that they wonder if that's your only reason for seeking a new job. Be prepared to discuss your current or previous base rate, overtime, bonuses, benefits, and forthcoming merit increases. However, avoid simply regurgitating your list of other demands (moving allowance, vacation, etc.) at the first opportunity. These differ from discussing pay. Be slightly coy and indicate that you'll share more specifics on what other considerations you're hoping for in the very near future. It's okay to go on record that to tackle this new role wholeheartedly, you'd like to see reasonable improvement from your current situation (after all, you might be giving up seniority, stability, or your residence to come on board).

If the offered salary isn't what you think is fair, most competent hiring managers are prepared to entertain a counteroffer. Consequently, you need to be ready to counter or attempt a compromise. Case in point, "If you can't offer me a 20% pay increase to start, would you consider giving me a six-month review, where an additional 10% increase would be available?" However, remember that "one in the hand is worth two in the bush" and that agreements to be handled in the future may be interpreted differently by your new (or worse, subsequent) boss. They may give you a review, but it could come with less than the increase you'd discussed, especially if some of the players have changed. Future agreements are best put into writing, such as an offer letter, even if only handwritten and signed on a scrap of paper. I've experienced this.

Most medium and large companies have job grades and salary ranges. Unless they're very small, they also have coworkers with whom they can compare responsibilities and salary. Both provide a degree of flexibility in formulating your pay package if you're not at or near a bracket ceiling. For your part, arm yourself with broad-spectrum information about what a job in your market pays (you can often research this online). This provides a sense of reality and allows you to be more intelligent as you successfully bargain.

Be leery of statements like, "We're offering you more than anyone else in this kind of a role." Does that mean you'll have difficulty getting decent raises in the future because you're near or at a salary ceiling? This goes hand-in-hand with trying to anticipate potential collateral issues and their impact. As mentioned earlier, when working for a summer youth employment agency, I was offered the head counselor position on an island pineapple plantation where I'd previously worked in the number two leadership role. I believed this offer to be a promotion and accompanied with a higher salary. However, because the facilities, conditions, and attitudes of employees (working directly for the agriculture enterprise) were sub-par, I asked to be reassigned thinking I'd become the head counselor on another island. Because I hadn't sought additional clarification, I was stunned to find out during formal staff announcements that I would be assisting a man I'd supervised two years earlier. Nevertheless, I stayed because I loved the work and the good we accomplished mentoring some of the troubled young men on our workforce.

Now, focus on the benefit portion of the package. Some benefits, like vacation time, may either be subject to hard and fast guidelines or have some wiggle room. *Note: I've found that if you've already made specific vacation reservations for the future, your new employer will accommodate these plans, perhaps as unpaid time, if you address them before accepting an offer.* If you determine they can't make allowances on a bargaining point, push a little harder for something else on your list. You're not going to get everything (if you do, please send me your contact information), but you should come away feeling like you did the best you could for yourself without upsetting the company's representatives. Identify the elements that are most important to you along with a couple you could live without, but would be nice. The same applies to a promotion or role change within your current firm. In this situation, you should be better positioned to understand which points aren't negotiable and would waste your time if discussed.

Next, scrutinize who you'll work with after starting your new job. It wasn't until I'd left one position and moved to a different state to run a distribution center that I learned the man who previously held this job had already been retained on a half-salary yearlong contract to consult. "Consult," my rear end. He came in about once a week, walked around for an hour or two, and then called the president whenever we made a change he didn't understand. This included taking potshots at the multi-million-dollar remodel design of the entire material handling and conveyor system just getting under way. To give you an idea, one day he called the president to tell him that boxes marked "pre-ticketed" weren't being expedited through the center. Of course, we received the next phone call. There was nothing wrong: the items had a barcode previously applied at the vendor, but our IT department hadn't yet recorded them into our database. Furthermore, no pricing was visible for the customers' convenience, so price tickets needed to be applied. You can imagine how happy I was when his year finally ended. If I'd known in advance, perhaps I could have negotiated some limits and conditions on his involvement, so it was less intrusive and more productive.

Lastly, a crucial warning: your spouse or significant other should never be discernably involved in any of the actual negotiations over job-related issues. This doesn't mean they can't meet the company's representatives, engage in small talk, join in interactions and pleasantries, or actively partner with you on developing negotiating strategies. However, their overt participation sends way too many negative signals, including that you can't speak for yourself. This rule holds even if they're employed by the same firm.

WHICH COMMUNICATIONS TO RETURN

Most of my career, I've tried to return every phone call I've received. Vendors who accounted for a large portion of the volume appreciated it. Over the last few years, I decided it was no longer prudent to continue the practice. Now I feel like I should respond to anyone I personally know, belongs to the same company, represents a vendor we've dealt with, represents a government agency (self-explanatory), or possesses a service or product my firm might need. I quit responding to cold calls from salespeople unless their pitch captures my interest. More often than not, I can't make out the indecipherable and often unintelligible call back number and rushed name and message they leave on my voice mail. If you need to leave a business contact a message, speak clearly.

If you're in sales, recognize how annoying it is to be left a message that doesn't indicate the purpose of your call. Avoid the shotgun approach composed of attempting to overuse business jargon and acronyms. Take the time to research a company first (see: "The Best Analysis Prevails"). If necessary, gather this information from someone who isn't the decision maker. You leave the worst impression possible if you spend the first minutes of a call trying to ascertain what the company does or what business model they're following. If your research has armed you with business intelligence, you can now take those first critical minutes to pitch your product or service instead. If you fish for insight, this is a red flag and may result in them ending the conversation while telling you to outline your firm's services in an email instead.

TIME OFF

A boss once told me that if I could leave for a two-week vacation, the company probably didn't need me. While away from work, a manager outside of my division asked whether my position was necessary. This happened when I'd traveled to Miami for my daughter's transplant, came back for two days to check on work and our other children, and then returned to Miami for another two weeks while our daughter lost the fight for her life. As you can see, being away for a long time can expose you even though you've worked hard to train everyone so things run smoothly.

Lao Tzu wrote, "A leader is best when people barely know that he exists, not so good when people obey and acclaim him, worst when they despise him. Fail to honor people, they fail to honor you. But of a good leader, who talks little, when his work is done, his aims fulfilled, they'll all say, 'We did this ourselves.'"[53] This is a noble approach, but be aware that some team members might not realize the culture and achievements you've fostered and think you're expendable. The alternatives to accepting this reality and what it results in are even less desirable. Among other things, they include abandoning teamwork and humility and can often lead to worse consequences like dishonesty and bitterness (see: "Take the High Road").

On another occasion, my supervisor asked me to call at least once a day while I was on vacation. While I honored this request for the eight years we worked together, I can't say I felt like I got to fully unwind on time off. While this may not always be necessary, it's wise to have key management staff reachable by phone or text if something critical arises. Personally, I've almost always limited long vacations to seven workdays (usually off a Friday, the next week, and maybe the following Monday). At one employer, when I qualified for a month-long sabbatical (an awesome benefit), I received permission to divide it into two two-week periods. Even then, I was somewhat paranoid I'd been gone too long, despite being on the phone a handful of times each week to check in. Always leave clear

---

[53] Laozi (Lao Tzu). *Tao Te Ching*. c. 400 B.C. Chapter 17. Translations of the original Chinese text vary.

instructions regarding any job duties to be handled during your absence (see: "Earn More Than We're Paid").

Regarding hourly employees, we had several attendance guidelines in place for a production-focused environment with line personnel: (a) generally, only 15% of staff could be on vacation at once, since other unscheduled absences increased the number of those not at work; (b) personal time off during certain busy periods—like the first three weeks of December—was not permitted, however, exceptions were made for events like births, weddings, and funerals; (c) because we functioned in a service-sensitive environment, three-day holiday weekends were limited to those when business was slow (like Christmas, New Year's Day, or Memorial Day); during busier periods (such as Labor Day, Independence Day, or Black Friday) when other divisions could allow longer weekends off (beyond the actual holiday), we granted floating days off to be used at other discretionary times; (d) requests were honored on a first-come-first-served basis and any ties were broken by seniority; and (e) vacations were limited to two weeks unless someone had an unusual need (visiting family out of the country, caring for an ill family member, taking an anniversary cruise around the world, etc.). *Note: Sometimes union rules are good guidelines since they represent policies your staff would generally prefer, and it prevents unionization because you already have some of those staff-friendly accommodations in place.*

On the other hand, time-off requests during holiday periods involving exempt employees (management staff) are scheduled on a rotating basis, rather than on seniority. This is especially helpful if you can't let everyone off. Say you have a long-tenured manager who always gets the week off between Christmas and New Year's while the other managers must work; this isn't fair and will ultimately cause resentment. Rotate popular holiday periods among your supervisory team but allow them to trade. You want policies that build the team, not destroy it.

HANDLING LIFE'S STRESSES

George Patton is the first person I'm aware of to be given credit for saying, "Fatigue makes cowards of us all."[54] Profound wisdom is contained in that short sentence. At some point even the strongest-willed mortals succumb to mental or physical fatigue. It's vital for each of us to know at any given moment where we fall on the continuum of high energy to absolute exhaustion.

I don't have all the answers on this topic, but I can share a few things that worked for me. During my early thirties I almost had a nervous breakdown, mostly brought on by a stressful job. It was at this time I began running. I found that my mind couldn't dwell on life's other pressures when I was thinking about how tired my legs felt or how I was nearly out of breath. Later, I focused on improving split times or enjoying looking at my surroundings (really). This gave my mind rest and since I often started to exercise around 8 or 9 p.m., it helped me to fall asleep easily.

Another coping mechanism has been to plan something each week that I would enjoy. This includes activities like hitting golf balls at a driving range, playing basketball, shooting trap, skiing, and going to a movie. It could be with someone else or by myself. It works because it's another form of pay for doing my job, in addition to the knowledge that I'm providing for my family. These weekly rewards make me feel like I can endure my job for several days because when the weekend or my day arrives, I get to participate in an outside endeavor I enjoy. Mowing the lawn, working on the house, or supporting church and civic activities also provide me relief.

Thank heaven for my wife who understands my needs in this area. I can recall a period of our lives when I'd go hit a bucket of balls at the

---

[54] Quoted in *Oxford Dictionary of American Quotations*, 2nd edition. Edited by Margaret Miner and Hugh Rawson. Oxford University Press, 2006. p. 258. Attributed to Patton's *War As I Knew It* (1947).

driving range, pick up a babysitter for our kids, and then go out to dinner with my wife after the early evening rush at the restaurant had subsided. By the way, family vacations and dates with my companion remain big life highlights.

At the top of my list, it also helps to have someone who will listen and allow you to get your worries off your chest. That has primarily been my dear life companion, but other family (including adult children) and friends have also been there for me. When I've felt unfairly treated, talking through it with a loved one is like letting the teapot whistle, a better tactic than building up all of that pressure inside. If you're an introvert this may require more effort on your part to find the safe space, people, or activities that bring you rest and happiness.

MAINTAIN BALANCE

Only a few years ago did I finally decide to turn off notification and text sounds (aside from calls) on my iPhone when home from work. I couldn't even sit through dinner without getting up several times to see what the problem was now. I certainly wasn't giving my sweetheart the attention she deserved, not to mention that I was keeping myself stressed by not providing time to decompress (see: "Multi-Tasking: Virtue or Vice?" and "Create Bridges, Not Enemies"). In response to these frustrations, I finally became diligent in labeling unwanted emails as junk. I've done fairly well organizing my email folders and items I no longer need, but I need to do better scheduling periods on my calendar for projects and limiting the times I respond to memos, texts, voicemails, etc. Manage your off-time work communication by pre-selecting a few times each evening or weekend when you'll check messages and respond. This keeps you in touch and shows you're concerned with carrying out your duties without working 24/7. I needed to compartmentalize the various aspects and demands of my life more. Of course, the exception to this would be if you work in a profession when you must be on call for emergencies.

A religious leader told me one of the secrets to life is keeping it all in balance. He suggested that to be successful, a person needs to be moderately good at being a (a) partner and parent, (b) provider, and (c) person (or Christian, in my case). He said he knew many people accomplished in business who were unsatisfactory spouses, parents, or members of their church and community. Furthermore, he knew many loving parents who nevertheless were inadequate providers and whose influence never reached beyond their immediate family. He also was familiar with community and religious leaders who neglected both work and family.

There are times when you need to stay late at work to get an important project done. There are other times when you need to leave work or civic duties to be with a family member in need. The trick is to be sensitive and wise enough to know when to do which. However, at the core of it all is valuing each appropriately. What good is all the money in the world if you lose your soul or your family? On the other hand—and I've been there—when you have a sick family member one of the most important things you can do to support them is to keep your paycheck coming and your medical insurance in force.

Experience tells me that I need a successful family relationship to help me get through difficult times. My faith, emotional health, and physical well-being have been heavily relied on to handle some of my larger trials in life. This includes the biggest of them all for my wife and me, the loss of our teenage daughter because of a chronic illness. We realize that others have experienced even greater suffering including the loss of entire families and communities. Sometimes we feel sorry for ourselves. My wife and I lost this dear child after a five-organ transplant. She'd been sick for ten years and on a transplant waiting list for three. About eight months after her death, my wife became ill with a similar malady. Due to health problems, my wife can't ingest much food because her small intestine doesn't work, and she has had some real health challenges ever since. Now we don't go out to dinner or travel like other couples, and her strength and vitality is limited. It's very easy to start saying, "Why us?"

When I heard a line from the movie *Tombstone,* it stuck with me and helped me put my own life challenges in perspective. While in a sanitarium as he lies in bed dying, Doc Holliday asks his visitor Wyatt Earp, "What did you ever want?" Earp says, "Just to live a normal life." Holliday replies, "There's no normal life, Wyatt, it's just life. Get on with it."[55] In this resides great wisdom. We would all be served well by taking this approach and not assuming that our lives are less because they're not what we consider normal or what we wanted them to be. Everyone is going to have challenges in life. No one is going to get through this easily. To me, that's because I believe we're on this planet to make choices between good and evil, which will determine what opportunities we're deserving and capable of in the life to follow.

We may look at a successful couple and see them living in a huge home, having all of the comforts of life, and little if nothing to discourage them. As a result we may say, "I wish I was in that position." But remember to keep things in perspective. They may not have a happy partnership and they may want children but can't have them. We may also find that down the road things have changed for those we once thought had life by the horns. Their situation might have altered dramatically due to poor health, failed associations, financial misfortune, or loneliness, just to name a few. There's wisdom from an old film: "Life offers you two precious gifts: one is time, the other freedom of choice—the freedom to buy with your time what you will. You're free to exchange your allotment of time for thrills. You may trade it for base desires. You may invest it in greed. You may purchase with it vanity. You may spend your time in pursuit of material

---

[55] "*Tombstone* (1993): Quotes." *IMDb,* 2023, imdb.com/title/tt0108358/quotes/?ref_=tt_trv_qu. Accessed 8 May 2023.

things. Yours is the freedom to choose, but these are no bargains for in them you find no lasting satisfaction."[56]

My brother pulled me aside when I was in my early twenties, feeling down, and trying to find my way. A girl I thought I might marry had just broken off our relationship. I was stressed trying to get through college and frustrated by going further into debt while working three jobs at once. He told me, "Don't wish your life away. Don't think you'll be happy when you finish school or get married or pay off all your bills or when you can retire."

Enjoy the journey. Count your blessings. This relates to a pearl of wisdom from Albert Einstein: "A happy man is too satisfied with the present to dwell too much upon the future."[57] In a similar vein, "It's not having what you want / It's wanting what you've got."[58] My formative years were wonderful, and it wasn't until I was grown that I realized how little we had. My youngest son spent two years on a religious mission in an area of Brazil where there's considerable poverty. He commented on how the children seemed to be so happy even though they had almost nothing in the way of worldly possessions. Look at the things you do have: your support group, your family, your friends, your health. Appreciate what you have and don't dwell on what you fail to possess. Give your loved ones the attention and affection they deserve.

We need to keep all aspects of life in balance if possible. Our physical, emotional, and spiritual needs require regular attention in order to complete life's journey in a manner in which we can take some pride and

---

[56] "Man's Search for Happiness (1986)." *YouTube*, uploaded by Hard-to-Find Mormon Videos, 1 Nov. 2015, youtube.com/watch?v=WbBIsxag5MQ. Accessed 26 May 2023.

[57] Einstein, Albert. "22. *Matura* Examination (B) French: My Future Plans." *The Collected Papers of Albert Einstein, Vol. 1: The Early Years, 1879-1902* Translated by Anna Beck. Princeton University Press. 1987. p. 15. einsteinpapers.press.princeton.edu/vol1-trans/37.

[58] Crow, Sheryl. "Soak Up the Sun." *AZ Lyrics*. 2002. lyrics.com/lyric/5444512/Sheryl+Crow/Soak+Up+the+Sun. Accessed 11 April 2023.

satisfaction. Years ago, I remember seeing a young woman who won an Olympic gold medal in figure skating appear on a football broadcast. They were interviewing her back when three celebrity announcers were in the broadcast booth. They asked her questions along the lines of, "How do you think the game is going?" and "Who is your favorite team?" Her reply was something like, "I'm sorry I don't know very much about football. I haven't had time to follow it. I've spent most of my life practicing ten to twelve hours a day and haven't had time to pay attention to much else." It was probably a surprising thing to say in a broadcast to millions of football fans, but it was the truth. She did achieve her goal. The question only she could answer would be "Was it worth it?" It probably was. More recently, an accomplished male swimmer decided that he had some catching up to do with other aspects of his life. Certainly, you can be dedicated to something, but you shouldn't do it to the exclusion of what really matters to you the most. Do your best in life and then leave the rest to fate.

In closing, I thank you for reading this book. I hope that it has been of value to you. If so, please look for the upcoming companion book, *More Concepts of Managing*, which offers additional principles to assist those further down their career path. I wish you success and happiness in both your work and personal life and would love to hear of your triumphs!

ABOUT THE AUTHORS

Ronald Harris retired as VP of Real Estate, Facilities & Construction at Young Living Essential Oils, having also served as Chief Logistics Officer. During his tenure, Young Living grew in annual sales from $60M to $2.2B and he assembled and oversaw the team constructing the 263,000-SF global headquarters, winning seven honors. Harris earned a Master's in Organizational Behavior from BYU and worked for seven firms with sales ranging from $90M to $3B and four with holdings equaling/exceeding these figures. He has an extensive breadth of experience in logistics, operations, retail, direct sales, construction, real estate, banking, agriculture, and taught at two universities.

Jacqueline H. Harris is a tenured professor of English in Idaho. She earned a B.A. from BYU, an M.S. from USU, and a Ph.D. from UNL. She has conducted and presented her research both nationally and internationally. Her publications include multiple peer-reviewed journal articles and book chapters.

Casey B. Harris works as an in-house counsel in Washington. He earned a B.A. from BYU, a J.D. from Lewis & Clark, and an M.B.A. from UIUC. He practices in general corporate, intellectual property, and regulatory law. His publications include multiple articles with the Association of Corporate Counsel.

www.ingramcontent.com/pod-product-compliance
Lightning Source LLC
Chambersburg PA
CBHW020647220526
45464CB00001B/329